DISCIPLE

A VERB

JONATHAN ENGBRECHT

ISBN 978-1-0980-2891-6 (paperback)
ISBN 978-1-0980-2892-3 (digital)

Christian Faith Publishing, Inc.
832 Park Avenue
Meadville, PA 16335
www.christianfaithpublishing.com

Printed in the United States of America

Contents

Introduction

Before departing, Jesus gave His followers this charge, "Go make Disciples of all Nations."

This Great Commission was His strategy for reaching the world with His transformational message and power! This same charge belongs to us today, those who follow Him, just as much as when He first spoke it to His original followers. Unfortunately, many today have lost touch not only with this critical mandate but also how this commission was meant to be fulfilled, literally the strategy for saving the world! Even within many evangelical churches that regularly preach on and prioritize the Great Commission, there can often be confusion.

Some think the fulfillment is achieved through short-term mission trips or evangelistic crusades. Others think it is achieved through a never-ending flow of more and better sermons, conferences, and biblical resources. Still others see it happening through peer-facilitated weekly small groups.

Now I am not saying that these approaches and activities aren't good or important. Quite the contrary, I believe strongly in engaging in all of these! The problem with these strategies, however, is they can easily miss the heart of the core strategy given to us by Jesus, this strategy being the one that He embodied and modeled for us with His own original disciples!

This book is meant to bring clarity and insight into this strategy not just in an abstract, intellectual way but to paint a picture of what it looks like for you and me to live this out, to not just be but also make disciples as Jesus himself did and called each of us to!

A Principled Approach

There have been several others who have developed books, trainings, programs, and tools for the purpose of discipleship over the years. Many of these contain some really good content, some of which I have recommended to others over the years, a personal favorite being *Master Plan of Evangelism* by Robert Coleman. This book is not meant to replace nor be a better version of some of those other great resources. Instead, I believe that this book meets an unmet need both in approach and audience.

You see, there are numerous books written for ministry leaders on how to build a discipleship program in your church through small groups or mentoring. There are other books that contain an exhaustive theological study on the subject in the abstract. There are still countless other books that are meant to help you personally in becoming a more mature disciple of Jesus through biblical study, spiritual disciplines, or evangelistic pursuits. Finally, there are yet others that provide a highly structured course or workbook for you to personally take someone else through in order to produce a disciple.

This book is different from all of those in that it is meant to be accessible not just by ministry leaders but by every committed follower of Jesus. It is not meant to be a program that gets implemented in your church, ministry, or even life. It is also not a highly structured discipleship course for you to lead someone else through. Instead, it is a model or framework for you to use in discipling others. It is a set of principles that embody the DNA or ethos of Jesusesque discipleship. This is not another "program" or "activity" for you to engage in. It is a lifestyle, mind-set, and set of values that should saturate your life. In the pages that follow, please do not view these principles as a set of boxes to check. Instead, let it be a springboard and guardrails for your own Spirit-infused creative initiatives for reaching and discipling those around you, wherever you find yourself or the Lord has you!

How to Use This Book

Fact: If you have truly been transformed by knowing and walking with Jesus for any significant amount of time, you are probably ready to play a direct role in fostering this in the life of someone else.

Some may read that last sentence and have a few immediate objections come to mind, like "I don't have time," "My church doesn't have a program for that," "What if I do it wrong, or that's not my specific calling." Truth be told, some of those are real hurdles, but none of that changes the fact that Jesus has called us to this good work—you, me and all the saints. For the moment, all I ask is that you put away any of these concerns and dream with me a little as one reason I wrote this book was to help you overcome these different obstacles, hopefully demystifying the process of making disciples. So just ponder for a moment what a lifestyle of making disciples of Jesus might look like in your life...

Are you a parent or guardian? There are unique and difficult challenges facing today's youth, in addition to the ones they have always faced, especially with regards to their faith. There is no better place to start this process than in your own home and with your own children. What would it look like to be intentional about discipling your kids?

Are you a student or athlete? You likely spend countless hours a year with the same group of people, many of whom you know are struggling in life and faith or who don't know Jesus yet. What would it look like to be intentional about discipling your fellow classmates or teammates?

Are you an employee? Most people spend the majority of their waking time working at their place of employment. In the United States, for example, it is not uncommon for people to spend well over two thousand hours at their job per year. Is there someone at your work you know who is broken, defeated, wandering, or without the Lord? What would it look like to be intentional about discipling your fellow employees?

Are you a small group leader or member? Do you see some of the same people in your church small group each week continually failing to understand their identity in Christ and God-given calling? What would it look like to be intentional about discipling someone in your small group?

Are you a ministry leader or pastor? You are at the tip of the spear for setting the vision and strategy for congregants to be discipled in your church. What would it look like to be intentional about discipling your staff, your lay leadership, or, even better, to help instill a reproducing culture of discipleship that ripples through your church and entire community?

Are you needing to grow as a disciple yourself? Have you been following Jesus but still wrestling with deep questions and doubts? Or struggling to have an impact on those around you or to pray or understand the Scriptures or even just trust God with the little things? What would it look like to be intentional about having a more mature believer disciple you?

Hopefully this short introduction has got you intrigued and excited about all the potential opportunities for impact all around you. By the end of this book, it is my sincere prayer that you know **what** a disciple of Jesus is, **why** you are called to make them, and **how** to start this adventure of making disciples right where God has you!

PART I

The What

Disciple: A Noun

A disciple is not above his teacher, but
everyone when he is fully trained will be like his
teacher. (Jesus, Luke 6:40)

A few years ago, I had the opportunity to speak at a church men's retreat. I was given complete freedom on subject matter for two one-hour sessions, which for me was a "kid in a candy store" type experience. For years, the content within this book had been stirring in my soul, having been field tested extensively in my own life. Now was the perfect providential opportunity to see if it would translate to others during this weekend event.

I didn't have to stir myself up to preach this message. Devotion to these truths had been a labor of love for more than a decade. Standing in front of the pulpit, I laid out clearly the biblical call and mandate for us to not only become mature disciples of Jesus but to radically walk alongside others and support their pursuit of this goal, that disciple was not simply a noun we are called to be but also a verb we are called to do!

I remember at the end of the second session I was talking to an older gentleman, maybe late fifties. I could tell that the truth in these messages had impacted him deeply but also that he seemed a little distraught. I asked him what God had been doing in his life that weekend, and he began to explain that he had been a believer for thirty years. He had faithfully gone to a good Bible-believing church, prayed, read the scriptures regularly, and tried to live a godly life. I could tell from the sincerity and humility in his words that he simply wanted to follow Jesus, wherever and whatever that meant.

At numerous times in the past three decades, he had been confused with deep, profound questions and feelings of abiding isolation, a wandering nomad in this struggle. He was faithfully doing everything he was taught for living the abundant life, but these abstract concepts and religious duties had not translated well for him. As I had been sharing, the reality had gripped him that in the past thirty years not a soul had come alongside him to truly model and support him in his quest to become like Jesus.

He wasn't critical nor was there any sense of blame. He simply was lamenting the fact that Christianity, done the way Jesus had intended, didn't have to be the isolated, confusing experience he went through for literally decades. At the same time, I saw a sense of relief that there was a better way as these struggles had clearly weighed on and strained his faith over the years. Looking into this man's eyes broke my heart, thinking of the unnecessary confusion and pain he had suffered for years like the victories that were never won, the gifts that were never unleashed, all amongst a backdrop of genuine love of His Savior and King.

In my experience, this is far from an isolated example and very likely the majority position. Too often, we celebrate spiritual births with great fanfare only to leave these spiritual infants on the side of the road with a bottle, box of diapers, and business card for the local spiritual nursery. That day confirmed for me beyond a shadow of a doubt that I had to do something alongside the many others passionate about this call to make disciples the old-fashioned way, Jesus's way.

I don't know about you, but sometimes I encounter ideas in the Bible that I find difficult to understand. I am guessing you might be in the same boat. This confusion can come from so many places, but it's often because we can't personally relate well to what is being said. Sometimes we lack the shared cultural or historical experiences and ways of viewing the world needed to clearly grasp the biblical meaning. This can be for reasons as straightforward as not being a first-century Jew living in Jerusalem when reading the Gospels.

This experience of "struggling to relate" is not unique to the Bible though as we all encounter this at different times in life. For example, I imagine you have met someone from a different culture, faith, or set life experiences and wondered at their unexpected and possibly strange words or actions. For me, one of the first times I encountered this struggle in the Bible was with the idea that we are part of a kingdom of which Jesus is king.

How do I as someone growing up in a Constitutional Republic, built around the ideals of individual freedom and autonomy, grasp what it means to live under the rule of a Cosmic King, in His Kingdom?

I have a good understanding of basic citizenship and patriotism but being a subject and servant of a king is something for which I have no context. Should I fervently study *The Lord of the Rings* or a few other medieval or fantasy films to try and grasp this? Even if they were good representations, and I'm not sure that they are, it still doesn't help me experience what it is like to live in a kingdom with a king. Unfortunately, our lack of understanding doesn't give us a free pass as we are still nonetheless called to participate in Kingdom life. I believe the topic of making disciples, which I shared about in the opening narrative, is much like this topic of the Kingdom. It is challenging to grasp because we can't practically or personally relate. For instance, can you recall the last time you heard or used the word *disciple* in a culturally relevant, non-churchy way?

Since the term *disciple* is outside most of our practical and cultural experience, before we can get into the details of making disciples, we first must know what one is. Before we discuss *disciple*, a verb, we must grasp *disciple*, a noun. That said, I encourage you to be patient with the first few chapters of this book as we lay this critical groundwork and foundation. The "action plan" will come, and there are plenty of thoughts for the "just tell me what to do" types. I promise it will not disappoint! For the moment, however, we must start with the basics and simply define this term *disciple* or run the risk of straying from our path. Personally, I have seen the lack of understanding in what a disciple is and how they are made result in numerous heartbreaking situations over the years, often principally identical to the one shared above. It is my prayer that, as you read this book, you will not only understand the term *disciple* as a noun (what Jesus is calling you to be) but as a verb that you experience daily in supporting others in this transformative adventure!

Not Just a Christian Concept

I often find it helpful when trying to better understand a term to first say what it is not. Specifically, the term *disciple* is not just a Christian word. It also does not relate exclusively to the twelve disciples of Jesus, another common misconception. Instead, this idea of "being a disciple" is one that has existed in a variety of cultures, through thousands of years of human history, from Plato to Confucius. We see this reality even within the pages of the Bible itself:

> Now John's disciples and the Pharisees were fasting. And people came and said to him [Jesus], "Why do John's disciples and the disciples of the Pharisees fast, but your disciples do not fast?" (Mark 2:18)

Not only did Jesus have disciples but so did John the Baptist, the Pharisees (a group of religious elites), and likely many others at that time. Perhaps the most important takeaway from this verse, however, is that a disciple is always attached to and known by their teacher. Here we find the foundation of the model, that you can't just be or exist as a disciple independently or on your own, you must be a disciple of someone. It is in this sense that there have been disciples and students of masters and gurus, spanning cultures and generations. Truly, as long as there have been wise teachers, there have been disciples to learn from and be named after their likeness.

A Simple and Profound Definition

In its simplest form the concept of a disciple is founded on the idea of transferring knowledge and wisdom from teacher to student. As our modern society has more access to knowledge than ever before, you might be thinking, *How can you say this concept isn't present within our culture?* We indeed have endless options for formal education and by the power of Google, Siri, and Alexa, I can instantly find the answer to almost any question anyone has ever thought. Yet the difference between this form of learning and being someone's disciple could not be more profound as the transfer of knowledge was incalculably deeper and richer than the simple and sterile relating of facts.

Again, a disciple is someone who attaches themselves to a wise teacher, master, rabbi, guru, or the like. They not only listen to the teacher relate information but they watch the teacher, study the teacher, discuss with the teacher, take correction from the teacher, laugh, cry, eat, and live with the teacher. All the while, they are learning to become like the teacher as the wisdom, lifestyle, skills, and even the very nature of the teacher is imparted to the student. So profound was this transfer from teacher to disciple that people could tell whose disciple you were by simply observing you. Jesus Himself said it this way in Luke 6:40, "The student is not above the teacher, but everyone who is fully trained will be like their teacher."

In our modern understanding, learning is something you do in the context of a school class or lecture. It is the simple communication and retention of facts and ideas. You have learned something when you can regurgitate it on an exam. The problem with this view of learning is that it is too narrow, too incomplete, as we are learning and being shaped as people all the time. This continual learning is most clearly seen in small children who start doing and saying what they see those around them doing and saying, not all of which is positive I might add. Many times, parents "teach" their children bad habits they themselves have, whether they intended to or not. It is this type of learning, founded in relationship and doing life together, that often has the strongest impact. Much of this form of learning also seems to happen subconsciously and not only shapes our ideas but our character and the very lens through which we see the world.

Most of us have experienced brief moments of this transformational learning when we recall key teachers, coaches, or friends that shared life experiences with us, modeling proper behavior and speaking directly to our desires and fears. It is also why many parents are concerned with who their kids hangout with as they intuitively know the power of this type of learning and how it produces change both for good and evil. The apostle Paul, in writing a warning to the Corinthian Church, shares this idea by saying, "Do not be misled: Bad company corrupts good character" (1 Corinthians 15:33 NIV). The main idea being suggested here is that being a disciple of someone is fundamentally and inextricably linked to the "discipleship process" whereby through an intentional, intense, and extended relationship, the disciple is literally molded into the form of the teacher.

Rediscovering That Which Was Lost

Unfortunately, this concept of being and making disciples has been largely lost in our modern day. Consider how almost all of what we call "learning or growth" takes place in a classroom or lecture setting and is focused on the conscious memorization of facts. With our busy schedules and online friends, the opportunities for someone to learn by doing life with and following another are, in my experience, slim at best. Unfortunately, due to the norms and pressures of this world and our culture, we as the church have adopted these other forms of learning as the primary and often only way we develop and mature as disciples. Yet this is not the method of committed Christ followers throughout the centuries.

Consider what Paul says to the Corinthian Church, "Be imitators of me, as I am of Christ" (1 Corinthians 11:1). Or how Peter instructs church leaders:

> Be shepherds of God's flock that is under your care, watching over them—not because you must, but because you are willing, as God wants you to be; not pursuing dishonest gain, but eager to serve; not lording it over those entrusted to you, **but being examples to the flock**. (1 Peter 5:2–3 NIV)

The important takeaway from this first chapter is that a mature disciple is simply one who has become like their teacher in character and mind-set and not simply the recitation of their ideas. Additionally, there is only one way that a mature disciple can truly be made, and that is in the context of intentional relationships focused on Christlike transformation. This is not to say that our current methods don't have value or a role to play, they very much do, but they are also inadequate by themselves at completing the work of making mature disciples.

In our desire to mechanize, streamline, and automate everything in our world for the sake of efficiency, we have tried to shortcut this learning process by removing much of the messy and time-consuming relational aspects of it in our schools, families, businesses, and even churches. Too often, we have collected countless facts about life but have failed to really learn how to live. We may have been told how to behave but may never have developed a deep character and moral compass from imitating another. We are often bombarded with thoughts and ideologies from politicians and pastors to YouTube videos and Instagram posts, often never developing the skills to reason and wrestle through these competing ideas to discern truth. And sadly, we often have no tangible model for how to help those that will come after us to experience something better. We need more disciples of Jesus!

Personal Challenge

At the end of each chapter, there will be a short personal challenge for you to engage with. Obviously, these are not mandatory to continue reading; but if you want to get the most out of our time together, I encourage you to set aside some time to engage with the material in each chapter either through these challenges or in your own way.

Spend some time reflecting on the different areas of your life, including things like school, work, church, friends, family, and sports/activities. Specifically, for each area, reflect on how you have seen the principles of discipleship outlined here affect them:

> What effect has their presence or absence had on you personally?
> What effect has their presence or absence had on those around you?
> What are some practical ways you think that these principles could be better incorporated into some of these areas?

A Disciple of Jesus

My little children, for whom I am again in
the anguish of childbirth until Christ is formed
in you! (Apostle Paul, Galatians 4:19)

*Have you ever found yourself with that inexpressible feeling that some-
thing is wrong but you can't quite place it? These types of feelings can
gnaw at our thoughts and peace in a way few things can, so subtle yet
always present. They are like a hidden splinter in the heart, in the mind.*

*Many years ago, I found myself in just such a place. I was doing all
the "right things," and outwardly all seemed to be going well, so well in
fact that I convinced myself that things were indeed quite well. This in
spite the fact that deep down, I affirmed this as falsehood. I still hadn't
found what I was looking for...*

*At this point, you might be thinking this is a prelude to my conver-
sion story; but as you can now guess, you would be wrong. I had already
been a fervent believer for many years, having had a radical conversion
experience during a time of deep brokenness and had seen the Lord work
in and through my life in countless powerful and awesome ways (a story
for hopefully another time). Even though I had been truly and wonder-
fully saved, redeemed, and set on a course to serve Him with the rest of my
life, a cosmic excavator was preparing to unearth some unsightly things
from my heart.*

You see, after years of living in this self-deception...

"How are you doing?"

*"I am doing quite well! Attending a great church, giving of my
time, talent, and treasure, leading and serving in numerous ministries,
all while holding down a successful job and committed to regularly praying and studying the word..." And on and on and on I would go describ-*

ing the perfect little world which I had created for myself based on the ideals I had been taught.

That was until seemingly overnight, it was all stripped away. A Job-like plague had touched my life, including my job, finances, friendships, family, ministry, health, and what was hopefully a future fiancée. It all shattered within a span of eighteen months, but worse than any of these losses was what it exposed within. Amid that experience, I still remember the haunting question that the Lord spoke to my heart, "If you never achieve another thing on this earth, is simply being with Me enough?" I knew the right answer, even the answer I wanted to give, but I realized it was a lie.

A deep bitterness and vengeful attitude had developed against those who had wronged me in that season. I would tell the Lord that I was done with the whole lot of them and that they deserved judgement to which He would reply, "I thought you said you loved them?" I would remind the Lord that they didn't deserve my love for what they had done, to which I could feel His eyes peering into my own heart. I was undone!

Somewhere in trying to live out what I thought was the "perfect Christian life," I had moved away from becoming like Jesus in spirit even though I had mimicked the form of the Christian life with extreme precision. I was one of those of whom the apostle Paul would have said he was still in labor pains until Christ had been fully formed in me. I thought I had known what it meant to be a disciple of Jesus; but in the depths of my heart, I had missed the mark. Thankfully, by His grace, the Lord started and continues to show me what it really means to be His and truly like Him, a disciple of Jesus.

A disciple, when fully trained, will be like their teacher; therefore, as people desiring and called to be mature disciples of Jesus, our aim is to be like Him, which is no small task I might add.

To be like Jesus, we must study and experience how Jesus lived to be transformed by His life. Fortunately, we have been given four separate detailed accounts of His time on earth in the inspired words of Matthew, Mark, Luke, and John. In studying these pages, there are numerous things that can be uncovered about the way Jesus taught, prayed, thought, and engaged with broken people of all backgrounds. Analyzing how Jesus lived His life could be several lengthy books on its own (John 21:25), and many such commentaries have been written over the years. That said, amidst the numerous stories and sermons of Jesus's life, a few fundamental characteristics arise which will be the focus of this chapter.

Note this will not be an exhaustive treatment of what it looks like to be a disciple of Jesus; and I, therefore, implore you to explore the life of Christ in detail through your own biblical study or additional good books on the subject. Not only that, but Jesus is alive and working in and through us and many around us, all the time, revealing Himself to the world! We have also been given His very Spirit to dwell inside of us, enabling the awesome privilege of being able to experience His heart and mind continually.

Jesus's Definition

In trying to determine the key traits that a disciple of Jesus would embody, a good place to start might be what Jesus Himself said. Specifically, there are a few places in the Gospel texts where Jesus points out the characteristics He desires and looks for in a mature disciple of Himself. It is these passages that we will focus on in this chapter, as again this is what Jesus Himself believes a disciple of Him should embody! These attributes are contained in the following three short passages:

> Jesus said, "A new commandment I give to you, that you love one another: just as I have loved you, you also are to love one another. **By this all people will know that you are my disciples**, if you have love for one another." (John 13:34–35)

So Jesus said to the Jews who had believed him, "If you abide in my word, **you are truly my disciples**, and you will know the truth, and the truth will set you free." (John 8:31–32)

Then Jesus said to his disciples, "**Whoever wants to be my disciple** must deny themselves and take up their cross and follow me. For whoever wants to save their life will lose it, but whoever loses their life for me will find it." (Matthew 16:24–25 NIV)

In the rest of this section, we will spend some time unearthing what each of these short but profound passages mean.

Love Others As I Have Loved You

Jesus said, "A new commandment I give to you, that you love one another: just as I have loved you, you also are to love one another. **By this all people will know that you are my disciples**, if you have love for one another." (John 13:34–35)

Jesus makes a remarkable claim in this first passage. The way our friends, family, community, and everyone else in this world will know that we are His disciples is not by our theological knowledge, moral purity, or religious observance but simply by our love for the brethren. At first glance, it doesn't seem that this mark of a disciple is very remarkable at all as many Christians seem to be "nice" to other people, and nobody seems to take much notice of it. I believe the reason for this is that we fail to understand was Jesus is really saying here. He is not saying that His disciples are simply to be nice to one another. His exact words are that we are to love one another as he has loved us! This begs the question, "How much does Jesus love us?" The answer being enough to leave the comfort, peace, and glory of heaven to step down into our broken and corrupt world and sacrificially give His life that we might have life more abundantly, expecting nothing in return, all while we were still sinful enemies of God. Now that's a lot of love!

A serious question for us to reflect on is, "Do we even love a single person with this much sacrificial love?" The answer for all of us is a resounding no. Now imagine a church where everyone loved each other with this same love that Jesus has toward us. It's hard to even imagine that such a thing is even possible or what it would even look like because it is so contrary to our nature. It is for this reason that Jesus says it will be the defining characteristic of those that are His disciples. You see, it is impossible for the world to believe this type of love could be real, without the miraculous power of God as its source!

Far too often, I have seen people in the church justify not fulfilling this commandment because of fear over petty theological differences or that someone's moral struggles might infect them or that they don't worship or observe Christian traditions with the same method and zeal. It is not to say that theology, morality, and spiritual traditions are not important; but according to Jesus, we will never become mature disciples and be shown to the world as such if we use these things as excuses to not love one another as He has loved us. Without embracing His example of sacrificial love, we will never become mature disciples.

Abide In His Word

> So Jesus said to the Jews who had believed him, "If you abide in my word, **you are truly my disciples**, and you will know the truth, and the truth will set you free." (John 8:31–32)

There are many Christians and churches today that place great emphasis on the Bible, the Word of God. In fact, today's believers, without a doubt, have the greatest access to biblical truth, more than at any other time in church history. With translations of the Scriptures in almost every language, Bible apps, online sermons, study tools, and weekly sermons all expounding on the sacred text, it would be hard to say that we are not in fact surrounded by God's Word. In several churches, people are also encouraged from an early age to memorize hundreds of Scripture verses on a whole host of topics.

Reflecting on all that, one might say that when it comes to abiding in Jesus's words, we are doing quite well for ourselves. Yet just as with the previous mark of a disciple, let's explore this a little deeper. You see, Jesus doesn't say that to be His disciple, you must be exposed to His words, have numerous copies of His words, discuss His words, or even memorize His words. He instead uses a very interesting term in how we are to relate to His words, and that word is *abide*.

To abide means to rest or remain in continually, literally, to have the Word of God living in the forefront of your heart and mind all the time, shaping and permeating your thoughts and likewise actions. Over the centuries, religious Jews have tried to accomplish this by attaching little wooden boxes containing scripture to both their heads and hearts when going about their day. This is clearly not what Jesus had in mind but gives a great physical picture of what should be happening within the souls of his followers.

Imagine for a moment that you and everyone in your church community let the truth of Jesus's words continually flood your hearts and minds. Again, this miraculous state of being is almost impossible to imagine. As His followers, we must not think that simply being near, reading, or even memorizing His Words are enough, or again we will never become mature disciples of Jesus. We must learn to abide in God's Word!

Pick Up Your Cross and Follow Him

Then Jesus said to his disciples, "**Whoever wants to be my disciple** must deny themselves and take up their cross and follow me. For who-

ever wants to save their life will lose it, but whoever loses their life for me will find it." (Matthew
16:24–25 NIV)

Sometimes as Christians, we can feel like we are being sacrificial
in following Jesus because we are fulfilling our religious duties. We
take time out of our Sunday morning to go to church or twenty minutes to read His Word and pray. Or if we are really going for broke
and putting it all on the line, we might leave our comfort and board
a plane to spend a week helping others on their spiritual journey in a
foreign country. The truth is that these, for the most part, are small
inconveniences, tiny speed bumps in the course of our lives. Even more
profound is that none of these really require us to lay down our lives
and trust Him and His plan for us in truly significant ways. Doing a
short devotional or attending a church service doesn't require you to
part with anything you really hold dear, except maybe a little sleep.

Jesus is calling us not just to part with a little free time but to
lose and put on the altar the very things in life we hold most dear
and trust Him and His plan. We are to follow Him in things that
are uncomfortable and challenging, picking up our cross, being ever
thankful that it is infinitely easier to bear than the one He carried on
our behalf.

Imagine what your life and that of your church community
would look like if everyone chose to deny themselves and trust God
and His plan for their life, no matter what the cost! Such a state of
being is almost otherworldly. As His followers, we must not be satisfied with a devotion of bearing simple inconveniences but rather
embrace our own cross and trust in His plan or risk never becoming
mature disciples and losing the very life we hoped to gain!

Compare and Contrast

Before moving on any further, I think it is important to compare
these three characteristics that Jesus gives us with what we might normally think of as the important marks of being a mature Christian.

Think for a moment about culturally what people typically consider "spiritual maturity" to be…

The following is my own "Top Ten List", in no particular order, of my experience of what is typically seen as spiritual maturity:

1. Attend a Sunday morning church service weekly.
2. Have a daily devotional time of scripture reading.
3. Give 10 percent of your income to your local church.
4. Attend a weekly small group Bible study.
5. Go on an international trip to engage in service projects or evangelize.
6. Have a daily prayer time.
7. Listen to only Christian music.
8. Don't swear, drink, or, in some cases, dance.
9. Obey the Ten Commandments.
10. Invite people to church who don't know Jesus.

Now I want to be extremely clear here, so don't miss what I am saying! I am not saying that any of the above things are bad or wrong. In fact, I think that many of the items in the above list are something that most mature disciples do and do well. That said, none of these things on their own or even all together mean that you are a mature disciple of Jesus. **The scary truth is you can do all ten of these activities consistently and not possess any of the three traits Jesus said are required to be a disciple of His!**

This idea might strike you as unbelievable, maybe even heretical, but consider just the aspect of Jesus calling us to love like Him in everything that we do. It is possible, if not likely, for us to complete the entire list of activities above with impure or selfish motives and therefore not be Christlike or mature disciples. The Bible is explicit on this point as it says:

> If I speak in the tongues of men and of
> angels, but have not love, I am a noisy gong or a
> clanging cymbal. And if I have prophetic powers,
> and understand all mysteries and all knowledge,

and if I have all faith, so as to remove mountains, but have not love, I am nothing. If I give away all I have, and if I deliver up my body to be burned, but have not love, I gain nothing. (1 Corinthians 13:1–3)

The actions recorded in this passage, I think we could all agree, are way more "spiritually impressive" than anything that we put in our top ten list. Yet the Bible declares here that without the Christlike nature of selfless love described earlier, I can do all of these amazing works and both "be and have nothing."

Even Jesus Himself points out how seemingly good actions, without the right motive, are not only worthless but can actually be sinful. In the Sermon on the Mount, Jesus criticizes the religious leaders of the day for **praying, giving, and fasting**—remarkable. The reason again is that they were doing these seemingly righteous actions for truly rotten and selfish motives, as Jesus exposes:

> Beware of practicing your righteousness before other people in order to be seen by them, for then you will have no reward from your Father who is in heaven. Thus, when you give to the needy, sound no trumpet before you, as the hypocrites do in the synagogues and in the streets, that they may be praised by others. Truly, I say to you, they have received their reward. But when you give to the needy, do not let your left hand know what your right hand is doing, so that your giving may be in secret. And your Father who sees in secret will reward you. And when you pray, you must not be like the hypocrites. For they love to stand and pray in the synagogues and at the street corners, that they may be seen by others. Truly, I say to you, they have received their reward. But when you pray, go into your room and shut the door and pray to your Father who is in secret.

And your Father who sees in secret will reward you… And when you fast, do not look gloomy like the hypocrites, for they disfigure their faces that their fasting may be seen by others. Truly, I say to you, they have received their reward. But when you fast, anoint your head and wash your face, that your fasting may not be seen by others but by your Father who is in secret. And your Father who sees in secret will reward you. (Jesus, Matthew 6:1–6, 16–18)

All of this is to simply say that we might need to realign our thinking of what it means to be a disciple of Jesus. We need to embrace the markers that He gave us and not what we wish they would be or what current church culture prescribes.

The Goal of Our Instruction

If you still think that I am overemphasizing Jesus's definition of what it means to be a disciple of His, a similar theme is related by the apostle Paul. In a letter to Timothy, his young pastor in training, Paul lays out what Timothy should focus on when training believers to maturity:

As I [Paul] urged you upon my departure for Macedonia, remain on at Ephesus so that you may instruct certain men not to teach strange doctrines, nor to pay attention to myths and endless genealogies, which give rise to mere speculation rather than furthering the administration of God which is by faith. But the **goal** of our **instruction** is **love from a pure heart** and **a good conscience** and **a sincere faith**. For some men, straying from these things, have turned aside to fruitless discussion. (Apostle Paul, 1 Timothy 1:3–6 NASB)

Here we have the same themes as the words of Jesus and a warning not to stray from them into things that don't produce spiritual edification. Paul tells Timothy that the aim or goal of our instruction is:

- ➤ **Love from a pure heart:** This clearly fits within the theme of Jesus's statement that His followers are to "love one another as He loved them." In becoming a mature disciple of Jesus, we must learn to love others as He has loved us.
- ➤ **A good conscience:** This fits within the theme of "abiding in His Word" as our conscience or thoughts are instructed and in accordance with His truth. Not that we simply know facts but our very conscience, which informs our actions and words, is good and therefore in accordance with His Word.
- ➤ **A sincere faith:** This fits within the theme of "denying yourself and picking up your cross" as this is the ultimate demonstration of a sincere trust and faith in God. You are saying I am no longer going to have faith in or trust myself and my plan but instead humble myself and sincerely trust and have faith in God's plan and calling in my life, no matter what it costs.

We must learn from Paul's instruction to Timothy and make the goal of our instruction to be these deep character traits from which many of the things within the Top-Ten List will overflow as Christlikeness is truly being developed in us!

Why Do We Stray

So the real question is why we seldom discuss the concepts of living out of sacrificial love, abiding in His truth, and trusting in God's plan through self-denial. Isn't focusing on these three characteristics significantly simpler than making sure we accomplish an endless set of "spiritual activities" like our earlier list?

I believe the answer is that although Jesus's words concerning what it means to be a disciple are simpler than the complex lists we often make, the activities and attitudes required are infinitely more difficult to fulfill. Said another way, if you had a choice between attending a weekly church service and loving others with the sacrificial love of Christ, what would you pick? Or if you had a choice between reading a chapter of the Bible every day and denying yourself or picking up the cross that Christ has given you and wholly trusting Him, what would you chose? That said, we must not be deceived and instead embrace these core characteristics of Christ or again risk never becoming mature disciples of Jesus.

You Are Unique

One additional note is that Jesus has made each one of us unique, and becoming like Him doesn't mean you lose that God-given uniqueness. Becoming like Him doesn't mean you must share the same favorite ice-cream flavor, sense of humor, personality, hobbies, or profession. These are given to you by God uniquely and are part of what make you special to Him and defines your role in His church. So no matter our profession, favorite ice-cream flavor, or hobbies, we should bring the love, truth, and faith of Jesus into everything we do. This is at the core of what it means to be a disciple of Jesus!

All of this Must Flow from a Love for God

Finally, to become a mature disciple of Jesus, everything we do must flow from a love for God. When someone asked Jesus what the greatest commandment was, His reply was simply to "love the Lord your God, with all your heart, soul, mind, and strength" (Luke 10:27). Truly this was the thing that marked Jesus's life more than anything else, His love for the Father. One might even say that this is the only characteristic of a disciple of Jesus as everything else we have discussed flows naturally from this wellspring of life.

The Epistle of John makes clear that the sign we truly love God is that we love the brethren! Jesus makes clear that if we love the Father, we would receive and love Him, the Word of God made flesh! Jesus also says that if we love Him and the Father, we will obey and likewise have faith in what He commands us to do. To be a mature disciple of Jesus, everything in our life must ultimately flow from a sincere love of the Father!

Personal Challenge

Reflect on your own current journey in becoming a disciple of Jesus. Here are some specific questions to guide you in this process based on our discussion:

> ➤ Are you growing in your sacrificial love for God and others, loving in the same way that Christ loved us?
> ➤ Are you growing in your faith or trust of God and His plan for your life, laying down your own life and learning to pick up your cross daily and follow Him, no matter what the cost?
> ➤ Are you growing in your knowledge of Him and His truth and learning to abide in His Word such that you see these truths affect your life?
> ➤ Do you presently or in the past more closely associate your own discipleship with the Top-Ten List or growing in love, faith, and a good conscience?
> ➤ How might you better embrace the Christlike characteristics discussed here in your own life?

PART II

The Why

The Great Commission

Now the eleven disciples went to Galilee, to the mountain to which Jesus had directed them. And when they saw him they worshiped him, but some doubted. And Jesus came and said to them, "All authority in heaven and on earth has been given to me. Go therefore and make disciples of all nations, baptizing them in the name of the Father and of the Son and of the Holy Spirit, teaching them to observe all that I have commanded you. And behold, I am with you always, to the end of the age. (Jesus, Matthew 28:16–20)

Having mentored many young men, for many years, you start to notice patterns in the things they struggle with. Having addressed some of the same issues time and again, I started honing little "talks" that I have on the ready for the next time that same situation arises. One such issue or struggle, which plagues most young men, is their inability to sacrifice the present moment for a better tomorrow. It seems that God has built this universe such that the things which are truly worth doing, providing the greatest impact and meaning, also require the greatest sacrifice! Said another way, the only things really worth doing in life are usually difficult. The sacrifice required to achieve these worthwhile endeavors usually comes in the form of denying yourself some pleasure today for something more lasting and joyous come tomorrow, next week, next month, next year, next decade, or possibly in the life to come... The best term I've come up with to describe this reality is "The Principle of Delayed Gratification," the forfeiting of a present desire for a more significant future.

The problem for most people, especially young men, is that it is hard to be motivated to sacrifice something you can see for something you cannot—to forfeit, for example, times with friends or watching sports to perform well in school by studying for an exam, an exam which will affect your grades and likely what college you get into, possibly even the degree you get, and ultimately what you may do with the rest of your life...

The temptation to embrace what we can have in the moment at the cost of our future is intense, whether it is forfeiting a stable financial future over the purchase of a frivolous item or sacrificing your purity and faithfulness to your future spouse over a one-night stand. In the end, however, regular surrender to our present desires almost universally leads to brokenness and regret, like Esau who sold his birthright to his younger brother Jacob for a bowl of stew. Later he passionately pleaded for that which he had forfeited, but it was not to be found.

When the Lord first led me to start investing significant time into a few young men, I was excited but quickly realized that the cost would be great. God would require me to invest my time, talent, and treasure, often with very little visible progress, some real heartache, and virtually no recognition. Thankfully, I had learned this principle of present sacrifice for future payoff in other areas of life. In fact, my faith in Christ was only possible because of Jesus's long and sacrificial investment in twelve young men in whom He had placed the fate of His church. What Jesus had accomplished with His investment in this group of ragtag misfits was the kind of future payoff I was willing to sacrifice for. That is not to say there weren't times when I wanted to give up or shirk my responsibilities or invest my time in something with more immediate results, quite the contrary.

Looking back, I am so very glad to have stayed the course. I have started to see the fruitfulness of steadfast, intentional investment in the lives of others, and it is truly remarkable. In addition to the impact it has had on their lives and the progress of His kingdom, I have also gained some of my best and truly lifelong friends through this process. God help us to sacrifice our immediate pleasures to invest in fulfilling such a Great Commission of making disciples!

In the last chapter, we talked about some of the core traits of being a disciple of Jesus. With that in mind, there is one more attribute, being at the heart of this book, that is also required as part of the maturation process of a disciple. This additional characteristic is "to make more disciples of Jesus." Put differently, a disciple of Jesus must make more disciples because making disciples is another important way we are to be like Jesus as He clearly commands us in this chapter's opening passage. **So crucial for the Kingdom was the process of disciple making in the life of Jesus that one could easily argue it was the single most important thing He did with His earthly ministry, save for the cross.**

If we are to truly be like Him, how can we ignore the thing he devoted the single largest portion of His ministry to? How can we ignore this Great Commission? So great a calling?

The Commission Dissected

The Great Commission that Jesus outlines in the above passage is something I have seen significant misunderstanding over. In my experience, many within Christian culture today equate the Great Commission with either a call to evangelism or global missions, specifically activities like short-term mission trips to remote places or evangelistic outreach events in the local church or surrounding community. As with many concepts covered in this book, traditional understanding is not wrong, just incomplete, as these activities are most certainly good and true. They are also definitely a part of fulfilling the Great Commission but are, just that, only a part of an even greater task! To help uncover the fullness of the meaning of His commission, let's break down the opening passage in some detail.

All authority in heaven and earth has been
given to me. (Matthew 28:18)

We see here that Jesus has claimed His place as king over both heaven and earth. While He was on earth, He preached the good news of God's Kingdom being at hand. After being resurrected and conquering death, He received all authority in both heaven and earth to see His Kingdom established in the hearts and minds of people the world over.

> Go therefore and make disciples of all nations. (Matthew 28:19)

Jesus then says, because He has this authority and desires to see His Kingdom established in the earth, that we, as His spiritual ambassadors, are to go in His authority and make disciples. We are to bring people into this spiritual kingdom, modeled after the heart and life of the king. Hopefully when Jesus says, "Go and make disciples," you now have a much better idea of what He is asking us to do. He is calling us to help transform both men and women of all ages and from every nation, tribe, and tongue under heaven to be like Jesus, our king, such that these newly formed disciples would love others the way Christ loved us, that their hearts and minds would be continually saturated in His Word, that they would lay down their selfish ambitions and trust God's plan for their lives, that they would invest their lives into making other disciples of King Jesus and that all of this would be motivated and flow from a pure love of the Father.

> Baptizing them in the name of the Father and of the Son and of the Holy Spirit. (Matthew 28:19)

Jesus instructs us that this discipleship process would begin with people publicly associating and declaring their allegiance to this new King and Kingdom. That in the waters of baptism they would symbolically die to their old way of life and the kingdom of darkness they used to belong to and just like their King be raised to new life, coming out of the waters of baptism a part of God's Kingdom.

> Teaching them to obey all that I have commanded you. (Matthew 28:20)

This last short clause is the part of the Great Commission that most often gets overlooked. Here Jesus is just emphasizing what it really means to make a disciple of Himself, that those who come into His Kingdom are to be trained as model citizens, being like and obeying the commands of the king, embracing the ethos, values and nature of the king, embodying this "law of the land" or the defining characteristics of His Kingdom on earth. It is ultimately this process, the process of building mature disciples or model citizens of the Kingdom that this whole Commission is about. It starts with them becoming citizens of the Kingdom as they trust in Jesus's sacrifice for forgiveness of their sin and the experience of new life, but it does not end there. As Jesus states here, the task is not complete until we have taught each other to obey all the commands of Jesus that we might be image bearers of our King!

Jesus the Mathematician

I'm guessing you've never considered the Son of God's math skills; but as we will see, He had a good working understanding of some key mathematical concepts. The fact that Jesus was good at applied math shouldn't surprise any of us not just because He was a carpenter but that He is also God, the one who created math. I know many reading this book probably hate math and that I'm in the minority of people who think it's cool, but I hope we can all get excited about this truly mind-blowing result from the Lord's application of mathematical principles in His world saving endeavor!

The Parable of the Growth Curves

To help some of you brush up on your math skills for this discussion, we are going to start by talking about linear growth. *Linear growth* is change that is consistent and constant, much like a straight line, hence *line*-ar. Most of us are very familiar with this type of growth, whether we know it or not. For example, if you are thoughtful about your money, you might put a fixed amount from every paycheck you get into a savings account at the bank. Let's say you get paid once a month, and you take $500 from each paycheck for savings. This would give your savings account a linear growth rate of $500/month. If you do this consistently, you will save $6,000 a year; and over a lifetime, you will probably have, assuming you started young and didn't spend any of it, $350,000 at the end of your life. This is linear growth.

Now for a little more complicated type of growth, the exponential variety. Let's say for this example you only put away $100/year instead of $6,000/year but that you put it in a "special bank" that was so good at investing your money it doubled every single year it was in there. Now I won't make you run the numbers yourself; but in just ten years of doing this, you will have almost $200,000. In fifteen years, you would have over $6,000,000! In twenty years, you would have over $200,000,000! In a lifetime, you would have more money than exists on the entire planet, again assuming you didn't spend it all. This is exponential growth.

Now I will ask you a simple question, "If you are saving money, is it better to have linear or exponential growth?" Since the goal is to "save" as much as possible, clearly the exponential growth is better! What you are really asking is, at the end of your life, would you rather have $350,000 to pass on to your children or all the money in the world? Some of you probably already know where I am going with this…

So, let's change our focus now from "saving money" to "saving people." Since the goal is to save as many as possible, in fact all the people in world, which is a better type of growth strategy? Linear or exponential? I think the answer to this is quite clear. Just like with saving money, you could see all the people in the world saved in your lifetime. I know you think that sounds impossible; but the great thing about numbers is that, unlike people, they don't lie. To show you just how powerful exponential growth is, let's think about another scenario.

Let's say that you led twelve people to the Lord every year for the rest of your life. Assuming you start early and live long, by the end of your life, you would have brought almost eight hundred people to a saving knowledge of Jesus, which is awesome to say the least! Now let's change the scenario a little bit and say you brought twelve people to know the Lord and trained them to be mature disciples over a three-year period, just one time in your entire life and then coasted and that, as mature disciples following in the Lord's footsteps, each one of these twelve people brought twelve additional people to know the Lord and trained them to be mature disciples over a three-year period and that this process continued from group to group, spiritual generation to spiritual generation. By the power of exponential growth, the **entire world** would have been transformed into **disciples of Jesus** in only **thirty years**!

You see, there were many times when the needs of the multitudes were pressing in on Jesus, and he seemed to walk by and ignore them in favor of spending time with His twelve disciples. We might see this attitude as callous and without compassion, but Jesus knew that the only way to effectively reach the whole world was through the power of exponential and not linear growth. What if Jesus had reached even ten thousand people with the gospel of the Kingdom during His lifetime but trained none of them to maturity as His disciples? The sad truth is that His ministry likely would have died within a generation or two of His death, not even being a blip on the radar of history. Instead, we should be thankful that Jesus was indeed a brilliant mathematician, understanding the power of exponential growth curves, and likewise invested the bulk of His ministry into the lives of twelve men. He knew the only efficient way to reach the multitudes was through transformational investment in the few!

You have now completed the mathematics portion of this book, and I promise you there won't be any more. That said, I hope from this you appreciate math more and how it impacts our world, as we have clearly shown it to be a vital tool in efficiently and effectively saving the world.

Long-Term vs. Short-Term Results

By this point, you are hopefully asking yourself why anybody would be satisfied with linear growth when there is this remarkable, beautiful thing called exponential growth? I think that there are a couple of reasons for this, although others may exist. I believe the first and most obvious reason is that people don't like math and have failed to apply its power to the problem of world saving. Jesus clearly did; so I guess one could also say that a small but important part of being a disciple of Jesus is embracing math, to which almost nobody said, "Amen." All joking aside, I believe the single most common reason is that we don't understand the trade-off of long-term investment vs. short-term gain. This is not unique to ministry, however, as was discussed in the opening thoughts of this chapter. It is a highly problematic reality that exists in almost every sphere of life!

To help illustrate these ideas, take the activity of spending one hour three times a week to exercise. Now most people don't enjoy putting their body through strenuous activity when they could be home watching their favorite TV show. In the short-term, watching the next episode of your favorite show, especially if binge worthy, is almost always more appealing and enjoyable than working out. Usually the only thing you get from working out in the short-term is an increased food bill, sweaty and stinky clothes, a gym membership fee, and a sore, achy body, especially as you get older. The long-term benefits though of regular exercise, compared with keeping up with your shows, could not be more significant. The benefits include more energy, less prone to injury and disease, longer life, enhanced quality of life, and better physical appearance. The problem is that, in the moment, it is hard to embrace this future satisfaction for temporary discomfort!

This same principle I believe holds true for the process of making disciples vs. traditional evangelistic strategies. Evangelism, when successful, can be an amazing rush! There are few privileges as great in all the universe as leading someone to faith in Jesus, as all of heaven rejoices with earth in these moments! It also clearly has the greatest short-term gains as someone has literally, in a moment, transitioned from spiritual death unto eternal life!

Now think about the process of making a mature disciple whereby you devote countless hours of sacrificially loving, caring, correcting, and supporting someone in the beyond-messy process of becoming like Jesus, often seeing little to no progress or even sometimes watching them move backwards. All the while, you could be spending a lot more of your time sharing the gospel with those who don't know Jesus and possibly see instant and radical results. You see, a purely evangelistic approach will always produce more and better results in the short-term. It is the discipleship approach (including evangelism) which, although not showing much in the short-term, has truly mind-blowing, long-term gains, as we saw demonstrated earlier. This is because in the first scenario, you are the only laborer focused on your task. In the second scenario, you are taking a large portion of your time to recruit and develop more laborers while occasionally laboring in the field of broken humanity yourself. In turn, these laborers also recruit and train additional laborers and so on and so on until you literally have an army of people working alongside you!

Discipleship is Jesus's Strategy for Evangelizing the World

I think that this is one of the most profound concepts needing to be embraced by the church today. We have literally tried every strategy and method we can conceive of to bring the saving message of the gospel of Jesus to the world. Whether it's crusades or outreach events, concerts or potlucks, evangelism training or short-term mission trips, gospel tracks or simply inviting people to church, we literally have tried it all, well, except for one strategy. The most ironic thing is that the one strategy we so often refuse to embrace is the very one Jesus gave and modeled for us. You see discipleship is not simply a Christian activity you participate in after coming to faith in Christ. Discipleship, understood and practiced correctly, is the best and most highly recommended (actually commanded) strategy given by Jesus for bringing His salvation to the world!

The sad truth is that our current approaches are even less effective than the linear vs. exponential growth curves would indicate. Since many in the church have not grown into mature disciples of Jesus, people don't see the message as being real, authentic, and truly transformational. Many people, who seem to have no problem with Jesus, don't want to come near His church because we appear to be nothing like Him. By not becoming mature disciples, we have lost the attractive and demonstrable power of the gospel that draws people to follow Him! By not embracing Jesus's commission to make disciples, not only do we forfeit exponential for linear growth but we also don't even get good linear growth because people don't see and experience the Savior through us. Discipleship is the strategy for reaching the world!

Important Clarification

Before moving on, I feel it vital to clarify what I have said in this section as some of it may have come off as overly critical or that I am recommending people to abandon traditional approaches to evangelism. Let me be absolutely clear that this is not my intent at all! I thank God for the countless creative, often Spirit-inspired strategies and approaches to effectively present the gospel to broken humanity. I praise God for those called to the ministry of an evangelist, who lead people to Christ in droves and equip the body of Christ to more clearly and effectively communicate the gospel message to people from every nation, tribe, and tongue, to literally become all things to all people that we might save some. Not only am I onboard with these approaches, I think we could even do more in this area!

What I am advocating for is a view of traditional evangelistic strategies as an integral part of a much greater and more comprehensive strategy for reaching the world with the saving power of Christ! It is not an "either/or" but a "both/and." This was the view of Jesus and apostles in their evangelistic pursuits, and I believe it should be ours as well. I hope that clarifies things for those who are specifically called, gifted, or passionate about preaching the good news to the ends of the earth. We should all love, appreciate, and thank God for your role and work in the Body. At the same time, we must not see the laborious, difficult process of discipleship as wasting time in place of these traditional pursuits, as the long-term payoff when we embrace both is salvation spreading to the ends of the earth, hopefully within our lifetime!

Personal Challenge

Reread the Great Commission, Matthew 28:16–20.

➤ How has this chapter altered your thinking on this great task and what you think about this awesome responsibility?
➤ How has this discussion affected how you see your own personal role in helping to fulfill the Great Commission?
➤ **Nerdy Extra Credit:** Think about a reasonable goal for your life in terms of how many people you can disciple, who make other disciples, including how long it would take, etc. Based on these parameters, calculate how many people your life could realistically impact (both directly and indirectly through those you have discipled) with the gospel in the next ten, thirty, and one hundred years by applying Jesus's strategy for reaching the world.

The Problem and Answer

For the wages of sin is death… (Romans 6:23)

My formal education and much of my career has been as an engineer. In the process of designing and building cool technology that has never existed before, surprise, sometimes things don't work like they are supposed to. When this happens, which is more often than I'd like to admit, engineers employ the process of troubleshooting whereby you systematically perform tests and analysis to better understand the nature of the problem in the hopes that you might ultimately fix it.

A critical part of this process is a technique called "root cause analysis." This technique allows you to get to the actual source of the problems you are observing so you can truly remedy the situation. A simple example of this would be if your car's headlights stopped working. The problem is clearly the headlights not turning on, but the important question when finding a solution is what is the actual or root cause of this problem. Some examples of different "root causes" for the same outward problem of headlights not working are burned-out bulbs, broken headlight switch, dead battery, dead alternator (charges the battery), etc.

The process of root causes analysis helps you determine which of these potential issues is in fact the underlying cause or source. For example, if you try and turn on the radio and it also doesn't turn on, it is likely the battery or alternator that is bad and not that the bulbs are burned out. Likewise, if the radio does turn on, it is more likely the light switch or the bulbs themselves which are bad. I hope I haven't lost anyone.

Without going into much detail, my life, like many people, has had numerous painful and challenging issues. Due to my engineering mindset, I tried for years to troubleshoot these problems and better understand their nature. Although I occasionally made some progress on a few issues,

46

it was clear that for many I had not successfully applied root cause analysis. I knew this was the case because my "fixes" to what I thought was the root cause never truly remedied the problem. The issue always came back or never really left. You see, I had proverbially placed new bulbs in the car, and the lights didn't turn on because I was unaware that in fact it was the battery that was dead.

After years of frustration and intellectual effort, the Lord was gracious enough to open my heart and mind to the truth. I had been trying to find the root cause of all the different sinful issues in my life and those around me. What I had failed to see was that sin itself was the root cause of virtually all of life's problems; but thanks be to God that in Jesus, I had the solution to this one!

As discussed in the last chapter, Jesus has given to us this Great Commission; and like any significant task, it is important to understand not only the what and how but also the why! So why is the "why" so important, you might ask. Simply put, it is where motivation comes from. It is the reason, the justification, the source of energy that spurs us on to action and fulfillment of the objective.

So why should we desire to play a part in this Great Commission?

I guess the simplest answer is because Jesus said so. This, in fact, is the only reason we need to know. That said, it is often helpful to also know the deeper reason behind a request, command, or mandate. I liken it to when your parents asked you to do something as a kid, and it should have been enough for you to obey simply because of who asked. Your parents might have even implied as much by retorting, "Because I said so!" In some cases, them simply asking wasn't enough, and you probably demanded the "reason" or "why" of the task. Now if the reason was good, I bet it made the task a lot easier to accomplish than being blind to or even confused by the purpose or motivating factor.

With this backdrop, we get to the central question of this chapter, "Why did Jesus entrust us with and ask us to fulfill this Great Commission in the first place?"

The Problem

Like most tasks, this one is meant to address a problem, in fact, a very serious problem, in actuality, **the problem.**

The Bible begins with people in paradise (the garden of Eden) and ends with people in an even more spectacular paradise (the new heaven and earth). The rest of the story is filled with pain, poverty, disease, destruction, and ultimately death. Now it turns out, after careful inspection, that there is only one variable that is different in the middle of the story as compared to its bookends which is sin and its consequences, ultimately the death of mankind. From this observation, it becomes clear that there really is only one problem from which all of life's ills stems, the problem of sin.

How big is this problem?

It is almost impossible for us to get our minds around how massive the problem of sin really is. That said, I hope to help you at least glimpse its gravity and weight. The following are just some of the consequences this problem is responsible for:

➤ For starters, the eventual physical death of every living thing…

➤ Every murder, rape, and theft throughout human history…

➤ The enslavement of untold millions of people…

➤ The fear of death that haunts each of us at some point in life…

➤ The countless number of cruel words uttered throughout human history…

➤ Every lustful desire ever conceived in our hearts…

➤ Every broken and strained relationship…

> ➢ Every ounce—more like metric ton, of human pride…
> ➢ Poverty, disease, genocide…
> ➢ Humanity's separation and war with God…
> ➢ **And that is the tip of the iceberg…**

To say that sin is a big problem is the understatement of time itself, being so large that our minds can't hardly grasp its destruction. Just imagine human history without the things mentioned in the above list, it would seem like, well, paradise. More personally, just ponder for a moment how much better life would be without sin and its consequences both for you and those you know. Again, this is only scratching the surface on how enormous this problem is but hopefully that gives you a small taste of its wicked depths.

It is not just Christ followers who have noticed this either, as wise and passionate people the world over and throughout all of history have dedicated their lives to solving this problem, whether they knew it or not, and virtually never at its root. Truly, every economic and political philosophy, every ethical framework, every religion, self-help book, and spiritual endeavor is man's feeble attempt at putting new light bulbs into a car while the battery is dead. This unbridled effort makes perfect sense though as when you ponder the above results of this root cause, there isn't really any solution or approach that should be "off the table" if it could truly solve this problem. Thank God He saw it that way!

The Answer

So what is the one answer to the one problem?

Yes, it is in fact everyone's favorite Sunday school answer: "Jesus." It is the reason that the gospel of Christ is beyond doubt not only good news but the greatest news of all time! Jesus came and provided the answer to the problem of sin which, as we have seen, accounts for more death and destruction than any person can contend with, let alone even comprehend.

So how did Jesus do it?

> And because of him you are in Christ Jesus, who became to us **wisdom** from God, **righteousness** and **sanctification** and **redemption**. (1 Corinthians 1:30)

Wisdom from God. Jesus is the answer, the actual embodiment of God's wise solution or wisdom to the problem of sin and its devastation on humanity. We experience this wisdom or solution to the problem in that Jesus also became for us the embodiment of our righteousness, sanctification, and redemption. We experience all these things when we are found in Him. If that seems a little abstract and deep, don't worry, it is, and we will be clarifying these concepts shortly.

Jesus is our Justification. (I was saved.) When Jesus died on the cross, He took on or bore our sin, literally became sin, so that sin and its punishment might be taken on our behalf. The Bible is clear that when we trust in Jesus's work on the cross, we are justified or made right before God. One of the simplest ways to think of this is in a legal sense where you were about to be justly sentenced for your crime until someone else stepped in and took the sentence and punishment for you, placing you in right standing again or justifying you before the law.

As a believer, when I placed my faith in Jesus many years ago, I received His righteousness and "was saved," being forgiven of my sins through Christ's righteousness and also received the future promise of complete salvation from sin and its ultimate consequence, death. Typically, when salvation in discussed in Christian circles, we are talking about it in this sense, whereby, at some point in the past, I trusted Jesus as my savior and was forgiven my sins, past, present, and future. As we will see, the good news is even better than we typically acknowledge as Jesus's saving work in our lives is even greater than this!

Jesus is our Sanctification. (I am being saved.) All of those who have trusted in Jesus for their salvation also know, even after

God has touched our hearts and we decide to only follow Jesus, that we often stumble and fall in many ways! We have numerous external and internal sins that we become readily aware of and often seem to lose the battle with. Our hope and prayer over time, as we have discussed at length within this book, is that we grow in our overcoming of these sinful passions and instead live in Christlikeness. The theological term for this process is *sanctification*, whereby our lives are regularly more set apart or holy, being more like Jesus.

Amazingly, the preceding verse indicates that in the same way that Jesus is our Justification, He has also become our Sanctification. He has given us both the example and the power, as will be discussed more in later chapters, to become like Him. Essentially you can consider the sanctification process as one and the same process as becoming a mature disciple of Jesus. The thing to note here is that Jesus has secured this ongoing transformative experience for us in the same way He did for our forgiveness of sins or justification. As we trust Him, we see Him continually saving us from our old sinful tendencies and passions while we remain in this earthly body, which is still sentenced to death. He condemned sin in the flesh. This sanctification process occurs in many ways but is ultimately empowered by His Spirit that lives within us.

Jesus is our Redemption. (I will be saved.) Just like Jesus, when I physically die, I will be raised again to new life, forever freed from the sinful desires within and the brokenness of the world around me. At this future moment, the salvation that started in my life when I first trusted in Jesus will be made complete. This is what it means that Jesus has become our Redemption, that He has completely and irrevocably delivered us from our desperate state of being bound to the problem of sin and its ultimate consequence, death. Again, it is Jesus who has secured this amazing victory for us and is the one who will complete our salvation by our future redemption, this being something our hearts should long for, like the apostle Paul.

> For to me to live is Christ, and to die
> is gain. If I am to live in the flesh, that means
> fruitful labor for me. Yet which I shall choose I

cannot tell. I am hard pressed between the two. My desire is to depart and be with Christ, for that is far better. But to remain in the flesh is more necessary on your account. Convinced of this, I know that I will remain and continue with you all, for your progress and joy in the faith, so that in me you may have ample cause to glory in Christ Jesus, because of my coming to you again. (Apostle Paul, Philippians 1:21–26)

A complete solution. As you can see, Jesus truly is the Wisdom or wise solution from God for the problem of sin. Through His life, sacrificial death, and resurrection, He has addressed every aspect of the problem of sin; and this is the gospel, good news. He has covered the penalty of sin so that we might be made right before God. He has given us the example and power to be transformed into His likeness while here on earth. He has purchased our victory over death and our complete freedom from the bonds of sin and its consequences, which we will experience upon physical death. Now if that is not an epic Solution, I am not sure what is!

So why is the Great Commission so great?

Simple, we are given the privilege to actively participate in seeing God's already-completed work of destroying The Problem being administered to dying humanity! Put more simply, we are called to be sidekicks alongside Super(God)man, helping to save the world!

You see, in Jesus, we have the answer to all the aforementioned problems—in fact, really any problem of true significance. In making disciples, we share the Wisdom from God with them, leading them to trust that Jesus is both their immediate Justification and future Redemption. We are then called to be vessels through which His purchased Sanctification can flow, working in glorious concert with the Holy Spirit, helping people to become more like Jesus!

Another beautiful thing is that as we experience the fullness of the sanctification or discipleship process in our lives, we in turn become walking billboards for the Solution to the Problem. The apostle Paul says it this way about those he was discipling at the church in Corinth:

> Are we beginning to commend ourselves again? Or do we need, as some do, letters of recommendation to you, or from you? You yourselves are our letter of recommendation, written on our hearts, to be known and read by all. And you show that you are a letter from Christ delivered by us, written not with ink but with the Spirit of the living God, not on tablets of stone but on tablets of human hearts. (Apostle Paul, 2 Corinthians 3:1–3)

Paul is essentially saying that their transformed lives were living letters of the testimony of God's salvation, again "walking billboards." Being a part of the Great Commission means we get to be a living embodiment of the life-transforming solution to world's most pressing problem and help others to partake. Hopefully that is a good enough reason and explanation of why we should embrace so Great a Commission!

Personal Challenge

> ➤ Think through the major issues and struggles in your life right now. How are they related to or have their foundation in the root cause of sin (either your sin, someone else's sin, or the effects of sin on this world from Genesis 3, etc.)?
> ➤ How has your understanding of salvation changed after reading this chapter?
> ➤ What have you learned about the sanctification process?
> ➤ How does salvation relate to the process of discipleship, especially the process of sanctification?

PART III

The How

A Work of Grace

And I am sure of this, that he [God] who
began a good work in you will carry it on to completion until the day of Christ Jesus. (Apostle
Paul, Philippians 1:6)

*A few years ago, I found myself standing in Wittenberg, Germany,
approximately five hundred years after Martin Luther had nailed his
famous or infamous, depending on your perspective, Ninety-five Theses
to the door of the Castle Church, as tradition maintains. It was at this
historic place and moment where we begin to see the seeds of grace that
the Spirit had planted in Luther's mind, which would ultimately lead
to the Protestant Reformation, without which I am not sure this book
would ever have been written.*

*Later that day, I was pondering the fact that the leadership of the
church in the Reformer's day had essentially taken grace hostage. It wasn't
that the grace of God wasn't available, just that the flow of that grace
was taught as only being available through the power and authority of
church leadership and, in many cases, for a literal price. "When a coin in
the coffer rings, a soul from purgatory springs," was the slick pitch of the
indulgence preachers in Luther's day as they literally sold salvation to the
frightened, broken masses.*

*In my heart, there was such a sense of gratitude for the liberation
of saving grace that had its genesis at this very place, not that it had ever
truly been bound except within the minds and laws of men. For the truth
of the gospel can never remain bound. For what ropes or chains can bind
a two-edged sword such as this?*

*As I continued to ponder these things, it occurred to me that although
the Lord's grace for justification through faith had mostly been liberated,*

the grace for sanctification seemed to still be bound in much the same way as justification had been in the Reformer's day. I began to lament how this seemingly missing truth of sanctification by grace through faith had negatively impacted my own life and those I had served over the years, the perpetual frustration I had lived with, my own inability to transform the lives of others and even my own soul, numerous passages of scripture shot through my mind...

> *O foolish Galatians! Who has bewitched you? It was before your eyes that Jesus Christ was publicly portrayed as crucified. Let me ask you only this: Did you receive the Spirit by works of the law or by hearing with faith? Are you so foolish? Having begun by the Spirit, are you now being perfected by the flesh?*

Since that time there have been numerous thoughts on the implications of this idea, and it will almost certainly lead to a book of its own someday. This thought was also part of the impetus for this book as this chapter, which covers several of its themes, is arguably the most important. This is not because it is the most critical as I would contend all the themes in this book are indeed "necessary." I believe it to be the most important because it is one of the least understood in the church of our day, maybe even in the history of the church... Over the following pages, I attempt to unlock a seeming paradox which, after countless hours of reflection and prayer, I think I finally have clear in my own heart and mind; and my prayer is that by, God's grace, it is clear in the writing that follows and ultimately within you!

We have spent a good amount of time covering what a disciple of Jesus looks like and that we are both called to be and help others become mature disciples. This chapter, however, will focus on what makes this miraculous process of transformation even possible. Understanding the principles in this chapter is essential as without them, everything else related to becoming and making disciples will have literally been for naught. We are talking about the truth that becoming and likewise making disciples is only made possible by God's grace!

Now grace is one of these words typically used only in Christian circles; and even there, many people don't really know what it means. There unfortunately isn't enough time to give anything close to a complete treatment of this concept but simply put: Grace is God giving us good things that we don't deserve. A few examples of His grace are the forgiveness of our sins through His Son, His unconditional love, adoption into His family, and His Holy Spirit. God doesn't owe us any of these things as we have done nothing good enough to earn them and done countless things that should have disqualified us. This is what is so amazing about grace! It is why the gospel, which means good news, is in fact such good news! God's grace has come and offered to us unimaginable gifts simply because He decided it to be so being the good, good Father He is!

Grace in Disciple Making

So how does grace relate to the process of making disciples?

I believe that the verse at the beginning of this chapter gives us a good first glimpse. Paul confidently asserts here that it is God who has begun a good work in us, the work of transforming us to be like His Son, and that He has an unyielding faithfulness to complete what He started. Note that the apostle Paul implies that God is the one who is ultimately responsible both for starting and finishing this transformative work within us. Since God is the author and we the undeserving recipient, this transformative task can therefore be considered an act of God's grace. Similarly, in the book of Ephesians, Paul repeats this idea:

> For by grace you have been saved through
> faith. And this is not your own doing; it is the gift
> of God, not a result of works, so that no one may

boast. **For we are HIS workmanship, created in Christ Jesus for good works**, which God prepared beforehand, that we should walk in them. (Ephesians 2:8–10)

Paul again points out that God is the one ultimately working within us and forming us into the likeness of Jesus. We are literally His workmanship or the thing that He is crafting, forming, and recreating in His image. There are many other verses that either directly or implicitly state that it is God that is forming us into mature disciples, saving us from our fallen state by His grace. So far, this might seem well and good to you, but now we have come to the point of contention and apparent paradox, the focus of this entire chapter. This confusing concept can be summarized by the following question:

> **If it is God who is ultimately responsible and the one who starts, empowers, and completes our transformation into mature disciples by His grace, what role then do we play in this endeavor?**

Clearly, we have a role as God calls us to both become like Jesus and, as part of His Commission to us (command), help others do likewise. The above passages, however, seem to indicate that this is God's job. Here we have what appears to be a contradiction, but thankfully the Bible directly addresses this confusion and so will we. My prayer is that, by the end of this chapter, you know with certainty what your role is!

Our Role vs. His Role in Discipleship

I think the best passage that describes how we work together with God in making disciples of Jesus can be found in the third chapter of Paul's first letter to the Corinthian Church. This is a long passage (vv. 1–15) and has a lot to discuss and reflect upon, so we will be taking it a few verses at a time. Here goes:

> But I, brothers, could not address you as spiritual people, but as people of the flesh, as infants in Christ. I fed you with milk, not solid food, for you were not ready for it. And even now you are not yet ready, for you are still of the flesh. (verse 1–3)

Immature believers. Here the apostle Paul is addressing the Corinthian Church whose members are still in the early stages of the process of becoming mature disciples. They are called infants in Christ and, even though genuine believers, are acting out of their "flesh," which Paul describes as our old, sinful nature (before Christ came into our lives). Paul is addressing people who have placed faith in Christ but are still in the beginning stages of having their lives reflect His.

> For while there is jealousy and strife among you, are you not of the flesh and behaving only in a human way? For when one says, "I follow Paul," and another, "I follow Apollos," are you not being merely human? (verse 3–4)

Jealousy and idolatry. Paul now turns to address the ways that they are acting immaturely, and the answer might surprise you. Paul calls them out because they are claiming to be disciples of their favorite celebrity pastor! Maybe you think Paul is a better pastor than Apollos or maybe someone else. You might think this is petty and ridiculous; but sadly we do this all the time in our American Christian culture, idolizing our favorite writer, church, preacher, or denomination. In some cases, we might even be jealous of members of a different church with a more popular and prestigious pastor. Paul calls this type of behavior worldly and a sign of spiritual immaturity. Lord, help us to grow up and out of these attitudes.

> What then is Apollos? What is Paul? Servants through whom you believed, as the Lord assigned to each. I planted, Apollos watered, but God gave the growth. So neither he who plants nor he who waters is anything, but only God who gives the growth. (verse 5–7)

Servants not stars. Next, Paul gives them a proper and mature view on the role of their spiritual leaders. What we tend to think of as stars, Paul refers to as humble servants of the Lord. Those who help to train us in the faith are obedient servants of Jesus fulfilling the roles that they were simply assigned. Additionally, each has their God-given role to play in facilitating the growth process, whether planting or watering, but that it is ultimately God that makes it grow. What we might think of as "spiritual stars" to be adored, Paul says, aren't much of anything as without God making it grow, their labor would be in vain!

> He who plants and he who waters are one, and each will receive his wages according to his labor. For we are God's fellow workers. You are God's field, God's building. (verse 8–9)

Divine partnership. Following his rebuke, Paul is clear to point out that God has called us to divine partnership with Him; and even though the specific tasks might differ according to our gifting and calling, we are fellow workers with God. Not only that but our jobsite is amongst fellow believers whom Paul calls God's field to be nurtured or God's building to be constructed. Each of us has a God-given role alongside what God Himself is doing.

> According to the grace of God given to me, like a skilled master builder I laid a foundation, and someone else is building upon it. Let each one take care how he builds upon it. For no one

can lay a foundation other than that which is laid, which is Jesus Christ. (verse 10–11)

Proper people construction. Next, Paul describes how people are properly built up or matured. Each of us has been given a different "section" to complete in the lives of others. Paul's role in this was to be what he called a "master builder" who laid the foundation of the gospel and fundamental truths of the faith in people's lives. Others were called to build upon this foundation with additional truth and encouragement as part of the discipleship process. Paul's warning here is that everything that is built must rest upon the foundation of being a disciple of Jesus and not producing disciples of yourself. It should also be noted here that Paul considers his calling and ability as a "master builder" to be an expression of God's grace.

Now if anyone builds on the foundation with gold, silver, precious stones, wood, hay, straw—each one's work will become manifest, for the Day will disclose it, because it will be revealed by fire, and the fire will test what sort of work each one has done. If the work that anyone has built on the foundation survives, he will receive a reward. If anyone's work is burned up, he will suffer loss, though he himself will be saved, but only as through fire." (verse 12–15)

Workmanship inspected. Here we finally grasp the gravity of Paul's warning in the previous section to be careful how we build. If we decide to bring people unto ourselves, built on the foundation of our stardom and opinions, we are building with materials of wood, hay, and straw. If we partner with God and point people unto the foundation of Christ and becoming His disciple, we are building with materials of gold, silver, and precious stones. Although some might enjoy building with wood, hay, and straw in this life, Paul says that there will be a day when God will test our construction projects. Note that those who build with poor materials will be saved but will suffer the loss of everything they built in this life! For those that built on the foundation of Jesus, their work will be preserved, and God will reward them for their service.

Pro-Tip: Build on the foundation of Jesus!

Key Takeaways

I hope that the previous passage was clear and helpful as there were a lot of deep and somewhat difficult concepts to grasp. If you are still feeling a little confused, I encourage you to reread the passage and the commentary again as these are critical and truths that are taught far less often then they ought to be. Additionally, I have provided what I believe are some of the key takeaways from this passage as a summary below.

> **The calling is by grace:** The apostle Paul makes clear that it is a gift of God or by His grace that we are called to take part in the spiritual formation of others. Specifically, Paul states that he is fulfilling a God-given assignment to be part of this task as a servant.

> **The ability is by grace:** The apostle Paul makes clear that the ability to perform his task was a gift or grace of God when he says, "By the Grace of God given to me, like a skilled master builder I laid a foundation." His ability to perform his task was by God's grace.

> **The growth is by grace:** The apostle Paul says that even with all we do as laborers, without the gift or grace of God to make the spiritual growth happen in others, we laborers do so in vain and to no effect. Specifically, he says, "So neither he who plants nor he who waters is anything, but only God who gives the growth."

> **Discipling is a privilege:** Since the apostle Paul makes clear that our call to disciple others, ability in discipling, and the transformation of those we are discipling is all a gift of God or His grace, then it would stand to reason that

God doesn't need us. And if God doesn't need us, then we should count the fact that He has invited us to this holy task and to participate in His family business as an awesome privilege!

> **There are no stars, only servants:** Because this is a privilege and everything is by God's grace, there can be no stars, except God. Thankfully we are privileged to get to work with a Star as co-laborers in the transformation of others to be like Jesus! And even though it is God accomplishing all of this by His grace, He generously rewards us for our faithfulness to the process.

It is vitally important that you keep these truths in forefront of your mind as we get into the details of making disciples, as we have a stern warning about how we are to build. We must not build on our own or another's foundation. We must not make disciples of ourselves but of Jesus. As Paul again says, those that build wrongly will one day suffer the loss of all their work…

Pitfalls of Ownership

Not only will nothing of substance be accomplished when we rely on ourselves to make disciples instead of the grace of God, but there are numerous pitfalls when we take ownership of this process. The list that follows are just a few of the more disastrous ones, being an in-depth lesson on what not to do. I can vouch from experience, having tried all these wretched approaches, as to how dysfunctional they can be. What I am outlining here is an all-too-common path to truly destructive behaviors that starts with the unassuming belief:

I am called to make disciples with my own strength to please God.

> **We view people as our projects:** From this core belief, people can quickly become projects, much akin to home-

65

work assignments in the school of discipleship that God will be grading us on. People stop being our brothers and sisters in Christ and instead "living tests and assignments" that we must perform well on to earn God's good grade and approval.

> **Relying on people's spiritual growth for your worth and value:** Since, in this wrong view, God is grading us on the spiritual growth and development of those we are discipling, our "grade" or performance before God is based on their success or failure. Since God is pleased with me based on my "grades," my worth and value as a person before Him is based on the spiritual growth of the person I am discipling. Let me just say, that's not a good place to be.

> **Trying to control people's behavior:** In order to justify myself and show my good works before God, essentially "earning the grade," the person I am discipling must act in a godly or spiritually mature way. Since they are sinners just like me, they don't always or even often do that. This causes me to ultimately try and control their behavior to preserve my "grade" and likewise worth before God.

> **Justifying ungodly means:** Since my reputation, worth, and "grade" is on the line, I am forced to resort to questionable means to try and produce change and growth in their life. Some favorite tools of the trade are guilt, shame, fear, punishment, bribery, etc. All of these things can be quite powerful in the short-term, producing "passing" external results. But the Bible is clear that all of these "tools" or "strategies" are not from God but rather the Devil himself.

Take it from someone who has tried: if you follow the above step-by-step path, you will not see any genuine transformation in the lives of others, at least not related to anything you are doing. That said, sometimes you might be effective in temporarily changing someone's external behavior to fulfill something like our Christian Top-Ten List from earlier. As we said before, this alone is not real discipleship; and even worse, it makes you and them believe that they have become mature in Christ when in fact no real transformational change has occurred.

Ministering out of this falsehood and pride often does significantly more harm than good. It also usually ends in severely broken relationships as nobody wants to be a "project" being controlled and manipulated by someone else for their own glory. Additionally, since it is not founded on the only true foundation that is Jesus, it will burn, and you will suffer the loss of these endeavors. I already know I will have some ashy heaps on my right and left when I pass through God's refining fire on that Day. I pray everything in your life survives this, the ultimate test of quality work! Never forget that external actions do not equate with real heart change, which again can only happen through God's grace!

Further Demystification

We have seen that the Bible teaches that we have a calling from God as laborers with a clear commission and mandate to make disciples of Jesus. At the same time, we are wholly unable to do this on our own, and to try is not only ineffective but can be quite damaging to ourselves and those around us. Additionally, there are many places where God states that He owns or is responsible for the completion of the commission He gave to us. We have also seen that God has given us grace or underserved gifts, empowered by Him to accomplish what He has commissioned us to do. You might still be seeing some confusion in roles. This is normal but do not fret as all is about to be revealed. At least that's my hope and prayer by God's grace.

Pressing on, we see that Paul was both aware and fully embraced this seemingly, paradoxical mystery when he says:

> For I am the least of the apostles and am unworthy to be called an apostle, because I persecuted the church of God. But by the grace of God I am what I am, and His grace to me was not in vain. **No, I worked harder than all of**

them—yet not I, but the grace of God that was with me. (Paul, 1 Corinthians 15:9–10)

In a single thought, he states that he both worked harder than every other apostle but that it was God's grace working in Him that accomplished that work. Confused still? This super important but somewhat difficult concept was one that I wrestled with for a very long time. It was while reading the following account in the Gospel of Matthew that my eyes were finally opened, and the Lord demystified how our two roles work together.

> Immediately he [Jesus] made the disciples get into the boat and go before him to the other side, while he dismissed the crowds. And after he had dismissed the crowds, he went up on the mountain by himself to pray. When evening came, he was there alone, but the boat by this time was a long way from the land, beaten by the waves, for the wind was against them. And in the fourth watch of the night he came to them, walking on the sea. But when the disciples saw him walking on the sea, they were terrified, and said, "It is a ghost!" and they cried out in fear. But immediately Jesus spoke to them, saying, "Take heart; it is I. Do not be afraid." And Peter answered him, "Lord, if it is you, command me to come to you on the water." He said, "Come." So Peter got out of the boat and walked on the water and came to Jesus. But when he saw the wind, he was afraid, and beginning to sink he cried out, "Lord, save me." Jesus immediately reached out his hand and took hold of him, saying to him, "O you of little faith, why did you doubt?" And when they got into the boat, the wind ceased. And those in the boat worshiped him, saying, "Truly you are the Son of God." (Matthew 14:22–33)

Here we see Peter do one of the coolest things a disciple of Jesus has ever done…surf without a board! So how did he do it? Well, he started by asking Jesus to command that he come out to Him on the water, and Jesus graciously agrees. Next, Peter, trusting in Jesus's Word to him, starts enviably walking on the water! Note that Jesus didn't force him out of the boat nor control his legs with each step he took. This was Peter's responsibility. The Lord did, however, make sure that Peter didn't sink by miraculously supporting him through defying His laws of physics. All was going well until the wind picked up; and Peter was gripped by fear, afraid that the wind was more powerful then Jesus's words and power. At this point, he began to sink, and Jesus was forced to pull him to safety, asking him about falling into doubt.

I believe this story perfectly illustrates the intersection of our role and God's role in many aspects of the Christian life, including becoming and making disciples. It starts with Jesus's command to us; but instead of getting out of a boat, the command is the Great Commission to make disciples, which is no less of an impossible task I might add. Jesus doesn't make us get out of the metaphorical boat. He doesn't control our legs. He simply calls, and we obey. The key here is our faith. Just like Peter, when we obey and start to attempt the impossible, we must trust that Jesus will make up the difference and perform the miracle, that He will work in and through us to bring transformation, making spiritually dead things grow. All will go well, and we will be "walking on water" in our discipleship efforts—that is, until we doubt in God's Word and ability in and through us, rely on ourselves, and sink amidst the crashing waves. Thankfully Jesus is always right there to pull us out and give us another shot at it.

The key to keeping our roles in the right place is to do our part by obeying Him but also have a heart of faith and humility in the process that Jesus will do His part, the miracle. This is the only difference between surfer Peter and soaking Peter, the state of His heart and mind toward Jesus. It is our faith and reliance on Him and His promises that enables us to accomplish this miraculous and impossible task of making disciples that He commissioned us to do. **Discipleship is only effective when we both obey God's command to do it and simultaneously place faith in His grace to accomplish it!**

Personal Challenge

When it comes to the concepts of grace and obedience, people typically error in one of two ways. Either they stay inactive, waiting on God to do and take care of everything, or they try and do it in their own strength for Him but without Him and His provision.

> ➤ Which side of this spectrum do you typically lean toward, and how has it affected your life?
> ➤ Reflect on a situation in your life that is currently out of balance in one of these two ways. What would it look like for you to both trust and obey in this situation?
> ➤ Have you been controlling toward someone in your life even if simply because you wanted to see them do the right things or grow spiritually? Pray through how you can approach them with grace and humility going forward and how best to heal any damage that might have been done already.
> ➤ Summarize what you have learned about the role that grace plays in discipleship.

Getting Started

In these days he [Jesus] went out to the mountain to pray, and all night he continued in prayer to God. And when day came, he called his disciples and chose from them twelve, whom he named apostles: Simon, whom he named Peter, and Andrew his brother, and James and John, and Philip, and Bartholomew, and Matthew, and Thomas, and James the son of Alphaeus, and Simon who was called the Zealot, and Judas the son of James, and Judas Iscariot, who became a traitor. (Luke 6:12–16)

When I first started discipling people, I didn't even have a word for what I was doing. All I remember was that the Lord had placed some younger believers in my life to equip and encourage in their sprouting faith. Funny enough, it wasn't until years later that it dawned on me that I had been attempting to follow Jesus's model the whole time. As I look back on some of those early experiences, I shudder at how I approached different aspects of the process. Truth be told, I had no idea what I was doing except what the Lord had put on my heart during times of prayer, and that was to help these young believers learn to follow Jesus better.

A few years ago, I was chatting with a couple guys who had participated in those early "experiments" in discipleship, and the experience of that time surfaced in the conversation. To my amazement as they reflected on that time, they shared how many of those experiences had forever impacted the course and trajectory of their life toward living for Christ. The only word that I could think of in this moment of bewilderment and shock was...grace! What I thought, in retrospect, had been somewhat of a train wreck, God in His goodness had used this simple obedience to touch not only these lives but numerous others. None of this changed the fact that I would have done almost everything differently except, of course, for stepping out when I heard the Lord's call.

When I started, I had no personal model, no method, no process… One of the reasons that I decided to write this book is that this is the book I wish someone had given me when I started. I hope you see from this story concerning my early experiments that it's not about having all the answers or doing everything right. It's about being obedient and doing the hardest part of all, starting.

I can tell you from experience that there are countless people whose hearts are longing, whether they know it or not, for someone to just care enough to walk with them as they learn to follow Jesus. For those reading this that have experienced this type of ministry, just think about what it has meant for you and your life. Now think about getting the privilege to be that for someone else, by God's grace. For those that have not experienced this, just think about a five, ten, twenty-year younger version of yourself sitting across from you right now. Would you have some important things to share with that person that could have helped them avoid some tragedy or change the course of their life? I would love nothing more than to be able to spend a week imparting wisdom to my younger self.

By keeping your wisdom, experiences, and life to yourself, you are likely sentencing someone else to repeat your struggles and fate without some much-needed support and direction. Hopefully, by the end of the chapter, I will have dispelled all of your concerns with getting started in what will likely be one of the most meaningful things you do this side of heaven!

Hopefully the previous chapters have encouraged and inspired you to think about how you can begin to fulfill the call of Jesus to make disciples, to come alongside others and share the good news of the gospel and help them become mature followers of Christ, to embody their Master. Sadly, many people reading this book have not had someone model this in their life nor have any idea how to start.

All is well though as we have the life of Jesus to reflect upon, His Spirit within to lead us, plus a few helpful hints in this chapter.

To begin the section on beginning, let's investigate the passage at the start of this chapter. This passage itself starts with Jesus spending all night in prayer. The only other time we see Him do this is before He is arrested on His way to the cross. In both cases of all-night prayer, it immediately preceded something important. Although we are not told the content of His prayers in this first case, what immediately followed was the selection of the twelve disciples. These are the ones the Father was calling Him to further teach, train, and entrust His advancing Kingdom to. One can rather safely infer that His prayers the night before were probably concerning those that would carry His name and message into the future, the world over.

In following His example, a good place to start is likely by praying for the Lord to bring people into our lives and show us those we are to teach, train, and care for. In fact, if you need to spend all night in prayer over this, so be it. You will be in good company. He might lead you to someone you know well or someone you don't know at all. He might even lead you to reach out to someone where it doesn't work out so well. Again, you would be in good company (Jesus selected Judas). The key here is obedience and trust that He will put someone on your heart and in your life, likely many someones, that you are called to nurture unto Christlikeness.

Before we get into the details of getting started, there are a few additional things to be aware of. Firstly, the people He leads you to may not always be the obvious choice in your mind and could even be the opposite of who you might suppose. This seems to be a consistent theme in the Bible, the most obvious example being Samuel's selection of David. Additionally, they might not be seeking discipleship or even know they need it, but that shouldn't dissuade you. I doubt that Jesus's disciples had any foreknowledge about the life transformation that they were about to embark on the day He called on them to leave their day jobs and come follow Him. Simply put, be open to the Spirit's leading and guidance concerning those He has called you to help disciple. With that said, let's get started Getting Started!

Overcoming Excuses and Doubts

It is said of many different tasks, the most difficult step is starting, which also often applies to disciple making. There are countless reasons people have for not beginning this process. Some concerns are legitimate and real, but many are not. In the end, whether legitimate or not, is immaterial because making disciples is a command of Jesus. Period.

Concerning roadblocks, there can be a belief that I can't participate because I am not prepared enough to do this, thoughts of, *"What if I make a mistake, say something wrong, or offend someone?"* The truth is we must all begin from a place of humility knowing that we will never be completely ready, and we will all make many mistakes! To help encourage you in overcoming the standard excuses and doubts, I have included a few important truths below. I hope these become safeguards for you to remain faithful in the process, as well as assist you in getting over that initial hurdle of getting started!

So what if I fail or mess up? *God's grace makes up the difference.* As we stated before the whole discipleship enterprise is a work of God's grace and where we fall short, we can trust God to make up the difference. Again, He is the only one that can truly change hearts anyway! You need to know that God is not surprised by your mistakes and that a few poor performances as part of your own growth process doesn't disqualify you. Just look at the life of Peter, whom Jesus entrusted to lead His church after His ascension. Peter messed up every task Jesus gave to him that we have recorded, except one, and even denied knowing Jesus after vowing to follow Him unto death. Yet God's grace abounded in the life of Peter; and a few weeks after his worst blunder, God used him to bring thousands into His Kingdom. Remember, where we are weak, He is strong.

What if I am not ready? *This process is as much about maturing you as the other person.* To become a mature Christ follower means you become like Jesus, who again, made disciples. Therefore, you learning to lead and guide others is a crucial part of God's work in helping you to become more like Christ. Know that this process of helping to make disciples is as much about maturing you as it is about maturing them. What this means is that you are never fully prepared to do this before you start as discipling is part of the growing and maturing process itself. If you want to become a more mature follower and better discipler, at some point, you will need to jump in and get your hands dirty!

Do I really have anything to offer? *Yes.* Even if you drop the ball in significant ways with the person you are discipling, I have found it helpful to return to this simple question, "Are they better off with you in their life or not?" The answer to this question is almost certainly yes; and as dumb as it might sound, something is better than nothing, and you are far more than nothing! You, child of God and temple of the Holy Spirit think you have nothing to offer… The value of your investment is especially important in our culture of busyness that squeezes out at every turn, meaningful relationships. You might be amazed at how consistently and genuinely just "showing up" in someone's life might appear to them as one of the most meaningful things they have. Don't worry about being perfect as your life is a net positive in theirs, especially since God is present and empowering the whole thing!

What if I don't have enough time? *Tough, discipleship is not optional.* The truth is that this is something we are commanded to do; and if you don't have time, you might have to evaluate your priorities and make some. That said, you also don't need to take on twelve people and live with them over the next three years. Maybe start with one person. Additionally, not all discipleship needs to be a multiple-year endeavor with tons of dedicated activities. There is much more in later chapters on some creative, time-maximizing strategies and different modes of discipleship. Stay tuned!

If you are still wondering if you can take that step to start, let me ask you a few questions that will hopefully remove any remaining doubt.

So what are you really being asked to do here?

> ➤ Can you care for someone?
> ➤ Can you serve someone?
> ➤ Can you pray for someone?
> ➤ Can you rejoice with someone?
> ➤ Can you walk through life with someone?
> ➤ Can you share with them what Jesus has taught you?
> ➤ Can you share with them what Jesus has done in your life?
> ➤ Can you encourage someone?
> ➤ Can you be a friend that helps someone else become like Jesus?

The big takeaway here is you can do it! Or more precisely, God can do it through you! If you are struggling with this, I encourage you to get over yourself and your inadequacies, trust in God's grace, and dive in!

It Doesn't Always Start with Evangelism

I think we have unfortunately confused the ideas of evangelism and discipleship in the modern church. Most churches, similarly Christians, see evangelism as a clear gospel presentation with the opportunity to lead someone to saving faith in Jesus. Discipleship is the activity that comes after, where we learn to follow Jesus by attending church services and having a regular devotional time, maybe even attend a Bible study. Although in many cases, this is how it happens, it's not the only way. Again, for a better-than-average example, look at the life of Jesus. When He called people to come follow Him and be with Himself, it seems clear from the gospel accounts that they didn't have a well-formed understanding of who Jesus really was and what His life was going to accomplish for the salvation of humanity. It was a process of getting to know Him and experiencing His life through which they came to really know and trust Him as the Savior of the world. (See Matthew 16:13–18 for more details on this point.)

To help get you thinking outside the box of the "standard process," I have included a few different scenarios, with people at different places and how you might engage with each, especially as it relates to the intersection of evangelism and discipleship.

The Christian. When you are looking for people to help become mature believers, the Lord might lead you to someone who has already trusted in Jesus or who is *saved* in the common vernacular. Over the years, I have encountered countless people who have trusted in Jesus but are wandering aimlessly, tossed around by the world and the devil, never reaching stability and maturity in their faith (Ephesians 4:11–16). In their heart, they desire a better way but struggle to perform the aforementioned Top-Ten List, never experiencing the abundant life that Jesus talks about (John 10:10). The great need to disciple believers in today's churches is an almost overwhelming thought but often gets overlooked for traditional evangelistic pursuits. As we talked about in the chapter on the Great Commission, these evangelistic pursuits, while good and necessary, can cause us to overlook the long-term strategy Jesus gave us in disciple making. Using a sports analogy, we have tons of potential star players sitting on the sideline, untrained or injured. The most effective thing we can do for the team is to get them trained and healed up so they can get in the game!

The ready heart. Sometimes you might encounter someone who has, by God's grace, come to the point that they realize they need saving and are ready to trust Jesus. If you encounter this situation, as the Spirit leads, share what the Lord has done in your life and for them on the cross. Share how the reality of the gospel has touched down in your life and can touch down in theirs. Give them opportunity to trust Jesus with their life and their salvation and then begin the process of helping them learn to walk out their new faith. Realize that someone in this state, although possibly well into adulthood, is a spiritual infant. They have been born again and can't yet even crawl spiritually, let alone walk. If you are discipling a young believer, do it as you would a young child, with much patience and grace. Nurture and walk alongside the individual, not being harsh with their mistakes as, just like an infant, they likely don't know any better. This is usually a labor-intensive process but one filled with immense joy as you get to experience their "firsts," first steps, first words, etc.—metaphorically, that is. This endeavor comes with both the difficulty and the pride and joy of being a new spiritual parent.

The open, but cautious. For someone who is open to learning more about Jesus but still not sure they want to take the plunge, we often apply pressure-based decision-making with traditional evangelistic approaches. These are not always wrong or ineffective, but again it is not the only way. In fact, Jesus was not this way with many people He encountered. Jesus's model was often one of letting the person kick the tires and test drive the vehicle, pushing it to its limits before buying. In this case, the decision is one immeasurably more important and life-altering than buying a car, house, or even choosing a spouse. High pressure sales is typically not the best approach for decisions like this, especially when talking with thoughtful people. Instead, we can start the process of showing people what it is like to follow Jesus before asking them to make a decision with life-altering consequences. We can say come let me show you what this Jesus is like and what it means to follow Him, to be like Him. Invite them to start experiencing His life with the hope and prayer that they trust in the one they have now encountered. It is in this way that the discipleship process can be begin, of learning what it means to follow Jesus, before trusting Him with your life. (If you want to study this a little more, some very informative passages are John 4 and Acts 17:10–12.)

The main takeaway here is that discipleship is for everyone and can start today! For some that the Lord calls you to disciple the evangelism component of their journey might have already happened. For others it might happen now or days, weeks, months, years, or even decades into the future. In all of these situations, our job is essentially the same, to point people to Jesus and lead them to follow and trust in Him that they might become like Him.

Breaking the Ice

Now let's suppose you have prayed for an opportunity, and you think the Lord has put someone on your heart to come alongside. What now? This is often the most difficult part for people and where they have some of the biggest qualms. I am here to encourage you that this part is actually quite simple, if you let it be.

All you are really doing is starting the process of doing life with another person in a more significant way and with a more intentional purpose.

So how do you start doing life with someone?
You start spending time together.
How do you start spending time with someone?
Well, you just ask them!

Many people think that starting this process must be some big formal and official, contractual thing signed as a sort of spiritual blood covenant. I can tell you from years of experience it doesn't need to be and is often better if it is not. It can truly be as simple as asking someone to grab lunch. From what we have recorded about Jesus beginning with what would become His disciples, the way He started was a simple invitation of, "Come follow me." Basically, come spend time with me. Let's get to know each other. Let's hangout, bro!

I have found that, like Jesus, this is usually the best place to start. Just get to know them and let the relationship develop as you are intentional with meeting and lovingly pointing them to Jesus. I have found that if, at some point, you do formalize the discipleship relationship, you are often just putting a name to or describing what has already been going on. This is not to say that you can't start by formalizing it, especially if you already know the person. It's just that this isn't a hard-and-fast requirement.

In conclusion, I hope and pray that you have not only been inspired, but all your excuses and fears have dissolved. And if that be the case, it is time to embark on the awesome adventure of making disciples. Even if the fears and excuses haven't dissipated, show a little Holy Ghost grit and, by God's grace, get'er done!

Personal Challenge

> ➤ What did you learn about the intersection of evangelism and discipleship and how they are related?
> ➤ What are the things that have held you back in the past from beginning the process of engaging in personal discipleship? Are these fears or obstacles valid; and if so, what is the process of overcoming them?
> ➤ Spend time praying for the Lord to give you one or more people that He is calling you to come alongside and help become more like Jesus.
> ➤ Come up with a simple plan (could be sharing a meal) to reach out to this person or people in a very specific way in the coming days and weeks.

The Process

Discipleship is a Jesus powered, messy, relational enterprise! (Me)

When I started this process some twenty years ago, again not even knowing what it was, I could never have envisioned the profound implications it would have on my life and those around me. When I step back and reminisce about all that has happened...

I remember the times when I would get the late-night or urgent calls, arriving to see one of these young men hopelessly broken over their sin, situation, or doubts with their faith, moments that required words of grace, hope, and sometimes hard truths that like rain would begin to wash their sorrows away, their tears often evoking my own...

I remember the hidden times of countless hours of prayer on their behalf that they would be mighty men of God, men of humility, wisdom, and courage, praying for the Lord to give me the grace to know just how to speak into their lives, praying for the Lord to intervene and take care of those that we loved when they were sliding into a ditch that I felt helpless to stop...

I remember getting to introduce them to some of my favorite activities and restaurants (I am a food lover). From camping adventures in the Colorado mountains and Minnesota lakes to climbing fifty-foot-high walls at the local rock-climbing gym to construction projects at our church's retreat center. As part of epic road trips or international excursions to Europe, Africa, and Asia, I have made it a habit to have one of them with me in almost everything I do. Life's classroom is anywhere you want it to be. I have taken Baptist kids to charismatic churches, suburban kids to inner city churches, and endless discussions around some of the most interesting and amazing food and beverages I have found the world over.

The best part in all of this is watching the transformation of their hearts and minds when they finally grasp a concept they had been wrestling with, enjoy a new experience, gain a new perspective, conquer a new mountain, or just share a moment with someone who cares about and believes in them!

I remember, more recently, as they have gotten older, not only being invited to their weddings but also standing up in them, an honor such as this I truly have no words for...

I remember hearing them tell stories of the adventures that Jesus had brought them on and how they have been used to advance His Kingdom the world over. From leading mission trips and local outreaches to seeing friends come to Christ, they have led Bible studies, preached sermons, run Christian camps, and been examples in their workplace.

I remember them telling me about the young men that they are investing in and the immense joy it has brought them, in some cases, more than anything else they have done with their lives...

I remember some of them like they were my own kids, who have grown into some of my closest friends, through countless adventures, with many victories and some heart-breaking defeats...

I remember a richness to life that I have not experienced in anything else I have ever done...

I look to the future for many more amazing moments with these dear friends and countless new ones that I have yet to even meet but that I trust the Lord will bring.

In this chapter, we will cover some of the key principles of how to engage in the process of making disciples of Jesus. Note that this is not even close to an exhaustive discussion but hopefully will provide a helpful framework for you as you embark on this adventure. Additionally, the next three chapters will provide some more practical details on what this looks like; so if you still have some unanswered questions, stay tuned.

Jesus Powered

As we discussed in a previous chapter, discipleship is only possible by God's grace, being empowered by Him. To shed some additional light on how this plays out, let's look at these profound words from Jesus Himself:

> I [Jesus] am the true vine, and my Father is the vinedresser. Every branch in me that does not bear fruit he takes away, and every branch that does bear fruit he prunes, that it may bear more fruit. Already you are clean because of the word that I have spoken to you. Abide in me, and I in you. As the branch cannot bear fruit by itself, unless it abides in the vine, neither can you, unless you abide in me. I am the vine; you are the branches. Whoever abides in me and I in him, he it is that bears much fruit, for apart from me you can do nothing. (Jesus, John 15:1–5)

Here we see Jesus make some extremely bold claims concerning our role as fruitful co-laborers. He paints a picture of Himself being the vine, the source from which life and nourishment flows and without which we would indeed be fruitless. If, however, we abide in Him, we will bear much fruit, and God will even spend time pruning the crooked branches out of our lives that get in the way that we might bear even more fruit.

There are countless Christians, you are hopefully one of them, that want to live fruitful and productive lives for Jesus and His Kingdom. Yet often in our zeal, ignorance, or pride, we try and do this for God, but apart from Him. The message of this passage is that if our sole focus is on being fruitful or just trying to bear fruit, we will produce nothing. Instead, our focus should be on abiding in Jesus; and if we do this, our life must bear fruit, having no other choice but to do so!

You see, if the fruit of our lives is the transformation of people into mature followers of Jesus, how do we ever expect to do that without Jesus Himself being present in our life? It is only through abiding or continually living with our hearts and minds connected to Him that His life flows in and through us, transforming and creating disciples of those around us. Just like Jesus was one with the Father and only did what He saw His Father doing, so we are called to be one with Jesus, that His nature might show through our lives. Simply put, it is impossible to make disciples of Jesus without involving Jesus and that the most central part of the disciple-making process is abiding in Him, that His life might radiate through us. If we abide in Him, much fruit is inevitable!

Relational (and Therefore Messy)

Few things have been as discouraging to me personally than when I compare the love and affection of someone like the apostle Paul to his fellow believers with what I witness in churches today. His relationship to the believers the Lord brought into His life was truly that of a father and brother. In many churches today, it feels much more like distant or estranged relatives. The nice thing about distant relatives is you don't feel much obligation to them, nor are you involved in the complexities and difficulties of their lives. Unfortunately, you also don't get to share in the immense joys of their successes or the richness of being their friend.

To demonstrate the relational heart and attitude we are supposed to emulate in the discipleship process, I have included some significant passages from the apostle Paul to those he was helping to become like Jesus. As you read these, contemplate what your church community or personal life would look like if this was the prevailing attitude.

> Just as a nursing mother cares for her children, so we cared for you. Because we loved you so much, we were delighted to share with you

not only the gospel of God but our lives as well. Surely you remember, brothers and sisters, our toil and hardship; we worked night and day in order not to be a burden to anyone while we preached the gospel of God to you. You are witnesses, and so is God, of how holy, righteous and blameless we were among you who believed. For you know that we dealt with each of you as a father deals with his own children, encouraging, comforting and urging you to live lives worthy of God, who calls you into his kingdom and glory... But, brothers and sisters, when we were orphaned by being separated from you for a short time (in person, not in thought), out of our intense longing we made every effort to see you. (Paul, 1 Thessalonians 2:7–12, 17 NIV)

I [Paul] do not write these things to make you ashamed, but to admonish you as my beloved children. For though you have countless guides (teachers) in Christ, you do not have many fathers. For I became your father in Christ Jesus through the gospel. I urge you, then, be imitators of me. (Paul, 1 Corinthians 4:14–16)

Paul, an apostle of Christ Jesus by the will of God according to the promise of the life that is in Christ Jesus, To Timothy, my beloved child: Grace, mercy, and peace from God the Father and Christ Jesus our Lord. I thank God whom I serve, as did my ancestors, with a clear conscience, as I remember you constantly in my prayers night and day. As I remember your tears, I long to see you, that I may be filled with joy. I am reminded of your sincere faith, a faith that dwelt first in your grandmother Lois and your mother Eunice and now, I am sure, dwells in you as well. For this reason I remind you to fan into flame the gift of God, which is in you through the laying on of my hands, for God gave us a spirit not of fear but of power and love and self-control. (Paul, 2 Timothy 1:1–7)

For some who are reading this, the idea of getting this involved in someone else's life is extremely uncomfortable, caring with this level of intensity, being this vulnerable, and exposing yourself to other people's struggles and them to yours.

I will not sugarcoat it. Getting involved relationally with people to this depth is very messy. It is much easier to show up to a weekly study and ask a few prepared questions than to walk through the roller coaster of life with others, to care for them in their hour of need, to remember them in your prayers, and long to see them that you might bring strength, wisdom, and encouragement. Many long for the ministry results of a Paul but only want to be one of the numerous distant guides or instructors in Christ, abdicating their roles as spiritual fathers and mothers. It is time to embrace the messy and get our hands a little dirty for the sake of the Kingdom.

Modes of Transformation

As has been stated directly and implied even more, there is no magic "formula" for making disciples as it is far from an exact science! We have seen thus far that being relationally involved and living out of an abiding relationship with Jesus are at the core of this process. That said, the rest of this chapter will focus on a few simple, practical, yet profound activities involved in making disciples. We begin this discussion by returning to a verse from the chapter on being a disciple of Jesus, whereby the apostle Paul summarizes our goal in disciple making:

> But the **goal** of our **instruction** is **love from a pure heart** and **a good conscience** and **a sincere faith**. For some men, straying from these things, have turned aside to fruitless discussion. (Paul, 1 Timothy 1:5–6 NASB)

Let us now examine each one of these goals or objectives in detail.

Instructing the mind (developing a good conscience). The apostle Paul says in Romans that we are to be transformed by the renewing of our mind. We must receive instruction about the truths of who God is and who we are in Him. Most importantly, we must faithfully revisit the truth of the gospel that we might live out of the knowledge of what God has accomplished on our behalf in Jesus. Therefore, one of our central duties in helping people become mature followers is regularly sharing with them and reminding them of:

➢ Who is God?
➢ What has God done for us through Jesus?
➢ Who are we in Christ?

There are countless formal and informal ways of doing this, ranging from an encouraging text message to reading and discussing theology books together. In our present day, the access to scriptural resources for you to use has never been richer. The important thing here though is to help them grasp and ever remind them of these truths as God gives you opportunity. As their minds are renewed to God's Word, they will fulfill Jesus's mark of a disciple of ever abiding and being saturated with God's truth! Again, it must be stated that the goal here is not simply the retention of biblical knowledge but that their minds would be captive to and governed by God's Word. Therefore, this instruction must always come back to the practical application of how these truths have touched down in your life and theirs.

In addition to sharing these truths with them, it is also critical that you teach them to continue learning and abiding in God's truth on their own. Your goal is not to be their eternal source of wisdom but to also train them how to study God's Word and depend on His Spirit for insight and guidance. Remind them of these great words that Paul spoke to his spiritual son Timothy:

> All Scripture is breathed out by God and profitable for teaching, for reproof, for correction, and for training in righteousness, that the man of God may be complete, equipped for every good work. (Paul, 2 Timothy 3:16–17)

Speaking to the heart (love from a pure heart). Just knowing the truth and even doing the right things is not enough. As we have seen, Jesus cares as much, if not more, about the heart and motive behind the action than the action itself. This is something we don't often talk about as it is significantly easier to focus on our external actions than what is going on inside our hearts. This is one of the most important things that we can address with those we are discipling as it is something that is often hard for one to see within themselves.

To illustrate this reality, consider that in Jesus's day, there was an entire group of zealous religious elites known as the Pharisees who knew the Word of God and engaged in religious activity that would make the most devout Christians today look like pagans. Yet these were so far from God that when He showed up in the flesh (Jesus), they killed Him. They had numerous books of the Bible memorized, made countless extra rules to keep themselves as far away from sinful activity as possible, and prayed long and eloquent prayers. The problem was that there was no love for God in their hearts, and they were only doing these things for themselves and for the praise and honor of men. In the disciple-making process, we can't forget to address the heart and motive of those we are leading or risk producing Pharisees and not true disciples. This point is so important that it will be the focus of the entire next chapter.

It is vital we do not forget that true disciples of Jesus aren't looking for recognition. Their reward is simply seeing their brother or sister blessed! They don't do good things for others to earn God's approval. They associate with the weak and lowly like their Master, even it if costs their social standing among pharisaical elites. They do things out of an overwhelming sense of thankfulness, gratitude, and genuine compassion for others. They live lives that are sacrificial in nature, not worrying about what it costs them, only the gain it provides to others. They not only forgive friends who ask for forgiveness but freely offer forgiveness to their enemies, even loving them!

Just like Jesus did with those in His day who had twisted and corrupt motives, we must address and confront these motives, bringing people to repentance. We must do this, however, with genuine humility, knowing that we are prone to the very same twisted motives. We must, by God's grace, be the spiritual eyes for our brothers and sisters, helping them to examine their own hearts.

The two most powerful, practical things I have found that help set our hearts in the right place, which you can use in the discipleship process are:

> **Praying for others:** Encouraging them to pray for others, especially those that they are at odds with, has an amazing way of rightly aligning hearts. When we go before God on behalf of someone else, God seems to perform heart surgery on us, helping us know His heart for them, thus realigning ours. It is hard to fervently and regularly pray for someone and not have compassion for them. In fact, part of the prayer can be "Lord, help me to love them and see them as you do!"

> **Reflecting on the gospel and worship:** The Bible says that we love Him because He first loved us. So often during our daily lives we forget how much He really loves us. There was literally nothing greater He could have done to demonstrate His love than His sacrifice on the cross! Reflecting on what that means through reading the gospel accounts, singing songs about God's love, or even remembering Him in taking communion are all amazing ways to revive that love in our hearts for God. As this love overflows within, it

will be the foundation of all our activities and help keep us from impure motives. These are great things to encourage and do with those you are discipling.

Finally, I implore you, don't take the seemingly easy road in this process and just focus on knowledge and obedience but also nurture and speak life into their heart! As those called to make disciples, we must comfort broken hearts, encourage the weary hearts, and correct the wayward hearts of those that we love in Christ!

Praying for and with (forming a sincere faith). The book of Hebrews makes clear that without faith, it is impossible to please God. (Hebrews 11:1) We must learn to trust God with every aspect of our lives, laying down our ambitions, and picking up our God-given cross. One of the best ways to engage in this kind of trust or faith is through genuine, heartfelt prayer both for and with those you are discipling. Prayer, as Jesus instructed us, is where we recognize God for who He is and also acknowledge our dependence on Him. We do this through words of praise and worship and by making our requests known, trusting that He will provide that which we cannot.

To help develop this faith, it is vital that you pray both for and with those that you are discipling as ceasing to pray and acknowledge our need for Him is to cease to trust Him and His plan for our lives. Jesus's response, when His disciples asked him about prayer, was founded in trust and humility. The prayer started and ended with acknowledging God as both our Father in heaven and ruler over all. In between these declarations, we make our requests known for all the necessities of life, which we cannot guarantee. We also ask for and trust that His will be accomplished on earth. It is through genuine prayers like this that we participate in a sincere faith.

To better grasp this idea of prayer leading to and expressing faith, reflect on some of the apostle Paul's prayers for the churches that he was discipling:

> For this reason I [Paul] bow my knees before the Father, from whom every family in heaven and on earth is named, that according to

the riches of his glory he may grant you to be strengthened with power through his Spirit in your inner being, so that Christ may dwell in your hearts through faith—that you, being rooted and grounded in love, may have strength to comprehend with all the saints what is the breadth and length and height and depth, and to know the love of Christ that surpasses knowledge, that you may be filled with all the fullness of God. Now to him who is able to do far more abundantly than all that we ask or think, according to the power at work within us, to him be glory in the church and in Christ Jesus throughout all generations, forever and ever. Amen." (Paul, Ephesians 3:14–21)

For this reason, because I [Paul] have heard of your faith in the Lord Jesus and your love toward all the saints, I do not cease to give thanks for you, remembering you in my prayers, that the God of our Lord Jesus Christ, the Father of glory, may give you the Spirit of wisdom and of revelation in the knowledge of him, having the eyes of your hearts enlightened, that you may know what is the hope to which he has called you, what are the riches of his glorious inheritance in the saints, and what is the immeasurable greatness of his power toward us who believe. (Paul, Ephesians 1:15–19)

Here we see Paul's absolute dependence on God, knowing that without Him involved, these believers whom he desperately cared for would not live victorious and fruitful lives in Christ. Praying like this both for and with those you are discipling will do amazing things to both instill faith in God and counteract our pride. Lastly, in addition to praying in faith for them and modeling this trust in God, regularly encourage this type of faith and prayer in those you are discipling, especially as they start to disciple others!

Modeling (demonstration). Concerning the aforementioned traits, often the best way to help people really grasp them is to model and demonstrate them. In fact, this approach was arguably Jesus's most effective. Jesus's whole earthly life was dedicated to revealing to us what God is like as He tells His disciples, "Whoever has seen me has seen the Father." (John 14:9) This practical modeling was also, not surprisingly, adopted by His followers as we see from the words of two of His apostles:

> Be imitators of me, as I am of Christ. (Paul, 1 Corinthians 11:1)

> Be shepherds of God's flock that is under your care…not lording it over those entrusted to you, but being examples to the flock. (Peter, 1 Peter 5:2–3 NIV)

You see, modeling is often one of the most effective forms of training as it often answers through simple actions what would have been numerous questions if it were simply described. Additionally, practicing what you preach has a way of lending credibility and inspiration to your words and removes mystery, having witnessed it being done.

When it comes to modeling, as we have already mentioned, Jesus was truly the master. School was in session with almost everything He did. His ministry was one perpetual object lesson, so our lives ought to be as well. In demonstrating what it meant to be His follower, nothing was off the table and no task too lowly. He had credibility with what He said because He was willing to do it Himself, even as the only begotten Son of God. I think we see this best in the following example from Jesus's life:

> Jesus, knowing that the Father had given all things into his hands, and that he had come from

God and was going back to God, rose from supper. He laid aside his outer garments, and taking a towel, tied it around his waist. Then he poured water into a basin and began to wash the disciples' feet and to wipe them with the towel that was wrapped around him. He came to Simon Peter, who said to him, "Lord, do you wash my feet?" Jesus answered him, "What I am doing you do not understand now, but afterward you will understand." Peter said to him, "You shall never wash my feet." Jesus answered him, "If I do not wash you, you have no share with me." Simon Peter said to him, "Lord, not my feet only but also my hands and my head!" Jesus said to him, "The one who has bathed does not need to wash, except for his feet, but is completely clean. And you are clean… When he had washed their feet and put on his outer garments and resumed his place, he said to them, "Do you understand what I have done to you? You call me Teacher and Lord, and you are right, for so I am. If I then, your Lord and Teacher, have washed your feet, you also ought to wash one another's feet. For I have given you an example, that you also should do just as I have done to you." (John 13:3–15)

In His life, Jesus modeled everything that we are supposed to do and to be, including laying down our lives for others. As you disciple people, realize that the world is your classroom, and there are lessons to be taught everywhere if we just keep our eyes and hearts open. Remember that in training others, you must be willing to do yourself what you are asking of others and that the greatest among you must be servant of all!

Giving opportunity (doing). Modeling is great; but in addition to showing them "how," we must also make sure to give them opportunities to put these lessons into practice. This is actually one of the most challenging things for many people to do, especially when it comes to something that they are responsible for or oversee. We must embrace the heart of John the Baptist when he said concerning Jesus that, "He must increase, but I must decrease." (John 3:30) Nobody likes the idea of decreasing or stepping back so someone else can step in. It takes us out of the limelight and the results of what the newbie does will likely not be as good as ours or, even worse...better!

The truth is that without good opportunities and constructive feedback from you, all the work you have done in discipling them will likely be wasted. They are not your competition, and you must see their success as really the fruit of God's work in and through your life! The hope is that we can say what Paul said of those He ministered to at the church in Thessalonica:

> And you became imitators of us and of the Lord, for you received the word in much affliction, with the joy of the Holy Spirit, so that you became an example to all the believers in Macedonia and in Achaia. For not only has the word of the Lord sounded forth from you in Macedonia and Achaia, but your faith in God has gone forth everywhere, so that we need not say anything. (Paul, 1 Thessalonians 1:6–8)

All of this starts with you empowering them by providing opportunities and setting them up to succeed. Jesus understood this and so after following Him for some time and watching Him model ministry, His followers were sent out by Him on multiple occasions with instructions to do what they had watched Him do. After their tour of duty, they came back and reported, discussing how it went so that the next time might be even more fruitful. You see, those you disciple do not exist to support your ministry, but instead you exist to support theirs!

The best prayer is that their lives are even more fruitful than yours as hard as that is for most of us to come to grips with. The truth is that as long as there are immature believers and those that don't know Christ in the world, there is much work to be done! So don't worry about working yourself out of a job as there is always more ministry to be done. Start giving others opportunity, replicating what the Lord has done in your life in another. This is the most fruitful thing you can do! At least that's what Jesus believed...

The Process Summarized

Hopefully you see that when it comes to the process of making disciples, there are only a few key principles at the heart of it. It begins with abiding in Jesus and that it is through your relationship/connection with Him that the power to transform lives flows. Without this grace of His life present in you, nothing will be accomplished. You must also be willing to engage with people in deep, genuine, and authentic ways, even if it gets messy, as this is often where real change takes place. You must not just talk the talk but walk the walk and model for them what it means to both be like and follow Jesus, to train their minds to be renewed in God's Word, to love others selflessly, and to live a life of sincere faith and obedience to God's plan and call. Lastly, you must provide opportunities for them to step out and implement what they learn no matter how awkward and challenging it might be. It is my prayer that this has started to demystify the process for you; but if you are still struggling with the practical steps, the next three chapters will hopefully set the rest in place!

Personal Challenge

- ➢ In your desire to be a fruitful Christian, do you tend to focus on abiding in Him or trying to bear fruit for Him but disconnected from the vine? How can you grow in your abiding relationship with Him?
- ➢ Spend some time counting the costs of what it means to truly engage in this process, specifically what it will cost

you in terms of your time, talent, and treasure? Are you ready to invest in someone with your very life?

➢ How have you done at modeling what it means to live like Jesus? How have you done at facilitating and providing others opportunity to grow in their faith using your own platform and resources?

➢ Think through some practical steps on how you can help people grow in their love, faith, and knowledge of God and try them out.

Older and Younger Brothers

> You hypocrites! Well did Isaiah prophesy of you, when he said: "'This people honors me with their lips, but their heart is far from me; in vain do they worship me, teaching as doctrines the commandments of men. (Jesus to the Pharisees, Matthew 15:7–9)

Throughout my years of studying the Gospels, of all the people that Jesus interacted with, those that have intrigued me the most are the Pharisees, the religious elite of His day. This interest primarily began when I was a college student at the University of Minnesota. For those that are not familiar, the U of MN is one of the largest universities in the country, with multiple campuses, the center of which is the Twin Cities, East Bank. This campus is home to dozens of buildings and at its heart a giant open grassy area, the size of a football field known as "The Mall." In between class periods, when school is in session, thousands of people descend on this area on the way to their next class to meet friends, read a book, take a nap, or as you might imagine some other truly goofy activities. The strangest one I ever saw was at high noon when six students ran, fully nude, across the entire mall as part of pledging for a fraternity. It was one of those moments where I should have looked away, wanted to look away, but just couldn't as one person tried to hurdle a bush and ended up doing a face plant into the grass, likely getting a pretty nasty rash...

During this season of life, one of the annual staples of intriguing "mall activities" was what became known as "The Mall Preachers." Like clockwork, in the fall and spring, a small but consistent group of Bible-toting (in actual holsters, I kid not) preachers would come to The Mall with a fire and brimstone "gospel message" that would make Jonathan Edwards shutter. (For those not familiar, Jonathan Edwards wrote a classic hell-fire-and-brimstone message called "Sinners in the hands of an angry God.") Shouts of whore, fornicator, and slut would gush forth from these pontificators like well-aimed missiles at the students passing by. Inevitably, a crowd would encircle these preachers and heated debate would ensue as condemnation and judgment over these students and their lifestyles would continue unabated.

At the time, I was a relatively new Christ follower and the message of the gospel, which might I remind you literally translates as "good news," did not seem to square well with the tone, tenor, and message of these mall preachers. Being the inquisitive sort that I am, on a couple occasions, I had discussions with these preachers about their approach and message. I have since forgotten the details of the arguments and passages they used in their justification; but the big takeaway was that Jesus Himself, on numerous occasions during His ministry, had harsh words toward sinners. This got me thinking even more...

Using the systematic thinking and training I was receiving at school, I worked through most of the passages where Jesus addressed people in their sin; and to my surprise, I found that His approach differed radically depending on who He was engaging with. To those who were found in the most clear and socially taboo sins like adultery, Jesus shared truth but typically with an abundance of grace and compassion. This example did not seem to be in line with the approach of these mall preachers to the morally loose college students they were shouting at. An even more surprising outcome of my investigation was who Jesus addressed with extremely harsh words and actions. From flipping over tables and wielding a whip to calling people snakes, white-washed tombs, and even sons of the devil himself, this sentiment was almost exclusively reserved for the externally pure, the religious elites of the scribes and Pharisees, who were inwardly corrupt with judgement and pride.

Reflecting on this, the irony was not lost on me that if Jesus had been there in the flesh, He might well have engaged in similarly harsh speech to that of the mall preachers; but to their surprise, it very likely would have been directed at them. This interesting observation that Jesus didn't engage with everyone in the same way puzzled me and made me wonder how I should best interact with people in trying to be like Him...

To understand that, however, I first had to understand why Jesus treated the woman caught in adultery so differently than the religious leaders of that day, a question from all those years ago that is the genesis of this chapter.

In the last chapter we covered some of the key principles of the process for making disciples. In the next chapter, we will cover some practical tools that I have discovered over the years, which have proven extremely helpful to the disciple making process, especially within our current culture.

In this chapter, we will discuss at length one such tool and insight that has been so significant and foundational, I believe it deserves its own chapter. And I guess, since I am writing this book, it in fact gets one.

To begin, remember several chapters ago when we discussed "The Problem and Answer." Here we identified that the reason we are in this mess to begin with is because of sin. Sin is indeed the one root cause from which all the wretchedness in this world flows; but thanks be to God that, by His grace, we are continually being sanctified, overcoming our sinful tendencies, and daily becoming more like Jesus, His disciples on earth—well, at least that's the hope! What we did not discuss in that chapter, however, was the nature of sin and how it affects each of us in unique ways. It is this uniqueness of how sin affects each one of us individually that will be the focus of this chapter.

One final note before we launch into this discussion. There are some significant, deep, and slightly challenging concepts and principles that I will need to work through before I get to the core content of this chapter. I have tried my best to condense and simplify this information as much as possible without losing much intellectual integrity. If you like philosophical musings, you are very welcome. If you do not, I would ask that you do your best to stick with this as I believe that the payoff in then end will be well worth the effort. Without belaboring this anymore, let's jump into the deep end together!

A Heart Condition

What is sin? This might sound like a strange question at first, but it turns out to be a very profound and important one. When this question is asked, most people's minds go to a list of some of the most obvious and heinous acts ever devised by man including murder, rape, theft, debauchery and, if you are an extremely conservative Baptist, dancing. Now it is true that all, well, at least most of these, are in fact sinful activities that are truly deplorable and expose just some of the many depths of mankind's wickedness. But I don't believe that this understanding gets at the heart, no pun intended, of what sin really is. To help uncover the nature of sin, we are going to get a little philosophical and ponder some weighty questions. So buckle up.

The first of these philosophical inquiries is, "Is it possible to sin without doing some form of action?" Many times, when we think about sin, it is in the context of many of the activities or actions that we listed above. This, however, is not a complete understanding as we will see from the passage below:

> You have heard that it was said, 'You shall not commit adultery.' But I say to you that everyone who looks at a woman with lustful intent has already committed adultery with her in his heart. (Jesus, Matthew 5:27–28)

Here Jesus presents us with a profound moral equivalence. He equates the unacted upon evil desire within our heart as being morally equivalent to having acted upon the desire itself. Just pause there for a moment and let that sink in. This implies that God views every wicked intent of our hearts with the same disdain and judgment as if we had acted upon it fully. Maybe I'm the only one, but this is a truly terrifying thought. But there's even more to it…

A second philosophical question, "Can I sin even when I am doing the right things but for the wrong reasons or with impure motives or heart?" If you remember all the way back to the chapter on "A Disciple of Jesus," we covered a passage where Jesus rebuked those that were praying, giving, and fasting because they did it with a wrong heart (Matthew 6:1–18). Or even more extreme, if you sold all that you had and offered your body to be burned as a sacrifice but without it flowing from a heart of love, it is worth nothing (1 Corinthians 13:1–6).

These passages and questions reveal an important and foundational truth about the nature of sin. Sin is, at its core, a heart condition and not an action, external thing, or worldly object. We know this because you can be immersed in sin without doing any external thing or even while doing what is typically considered to be godly activities that are commanded by God.

One last thought here which you might be asking yourself is why does God consider unacted desires of the heart to be morally equivalent to the action itself? This is not intuitively obvious as I think that most of us believe and live our lives as if they are not. This is probably not good, to view sin differently than God does.

I think that the answer to this question can be unearthed with one final philosophical question, "Why don't we often act on the evil desires of our heart?" If it is what we really want, the true desire of our heart, what prevents us from doing it? Literally hold sin's expression and manifestation at bay?

If you contemplate this question long enough, you will probably realize that it is the potential negative consequences that will likely befall us if we do act on these sinful desires. God views them as equivalent, the action and desire, because if all undesired consequences to us were removed, we wouldn't hesitate to act, so that the only thing keeping the expression of sin contained is our own selfishness. You can also prove this to yourself from experience and history. During city riots, people who have never stolen a thing in their life suddenly take numerous possessions from others because they know that they likely will not be caught. Or consider the times when you have acted on sinful impulses. Is it not generally when you find yourself in a situation where you are certain you won't get caught? Alas, we must move on to some more deep thoughts.

Morality of "Stuff"

Not to belabor the details on the nature of sin; but it must also be pointed out that, generally speaking, "stuff" is not evil. Throughout my life, it has become clear that many people view sin as something external trying to attack us. It is something "out there" trying to get in, and we must protect ourselves from the sinful things of this world. I want to challenge you that Jesus did not see it this way as you will hopefully glean from the following passage:

> And He [Jesus] called the people to him again and said to them, "Hear me, all of you, and understand: There is nothing outside a person that by going into him can defile him, but the things that come out of a person are what defile him." And when he had entered the house and left the people, his disciples asked him about the parable. And he said to them, "Then are you also without understanding? Do you not see that whatever goes into a person from outside cannot defile him, since it enters not his heart but his stomach, and is expelled?" (Thus he declared all foods clean.) And he said, "What comes out of a person is what defiles him. For from within, out of the heart of man, come evil thoughts, sexual immorality, theft, murder, adultery, coveting, wickedness, deceit, sensuality, envy, slander, pride, foolishness. All these evil things come from within, and they defile a person." (Jesus, Mark 7:14–23)

To help illuminate this concept, harken back to Genesis 1 where everything God made was "good," except for people which were "very good." This brings up other philosophical questions, "If everything God created was good, why is there evil in the world? And if God created everything, must not He also have created evil?" And similarly, "If God is purely good, how could He have created evil things?" Unfortunately, we don't have time for a complete dissection of these theological issues; but in cutting to the chase, God did not create evil things! Evil comes in the form of our hearts misusing and abusing the good things that God has made in self-serving and impure ways. So many Christians see the "things" themselves as the sources of evil, like alcohol or certain musical genres or, in some cases, technology as in the Amish.

The truth is that God made all things for good but in our hearts we choose to use them for things other than His good intent and pleasure. Take alcohol, for example. Without even addressing whether it is permissible to drink, this liquid can be used to clean and disinfect wounds, but the human heart often uses it to lose our better inhibitions and act in all sorts of perverse ways.

Another way of thinking about this is to take something as benign and necessary as water. Water is literally essential for vibrant and healthy life but, within the grips of a twisted human heart, can be used to torture and kill people. So are we to do away with water? Do away with everything because it can be used for perverse and twisted things? Where does the insanity stop?

> Let no one say when he is tempted, "I am being tempted by God," for God cannot be tempted with evil, and he himself tempts no one. But each person is tempted when he is lured and enticed by his own desire. Then desire when it has conceived gives birth to sin, and sin when it is fully grown brings forth death. Do not be deceived, my beloved brothers. Every good gift and every perfect gift is from above, coming down from the Father of lights, with whom there is no variation or shadow due to change. (James 1:13–17)

You see here again, in no uncertain terms that sin, at its root, is a condition and state of the human heart. It is in fact capable of corrupting everything in this world, even the good things given to us by God. This is the true nature of sin. We must not fail to understand this nature, or we will never be able to truly become like Jesus or support others in that process. This ends most of our philosophical musings. Feel free now to move about the cabin.

The Parable of the Older Brother

In this section, we will explore the different ways in which the sinful condition of our heart expresses itself uniquely in each person. Many of you are probably familiar with Jesus's parable in Luke 15, typically known as the Parable of the Prodigal Son. This title is not a part of the original text; and although these Bible headings are usually useful, this one is unfortunately somewhat misleading. There are three major characters in this parable including the father, older brother, and younger brother (prodigal); and as you will see, one can make a good case that the most important character to the main point of the parable is the older brother. If this topic interests you, Tim Keller has written an excellent short book on this subject called *The Prodigal God.* Before we get into pulling the principles out of this parable, I encourage you to read it in its entirety, preferably at least twice, to really get the details in your mind for the discussion that follows.

> And He [Jesus] said, "There was a man who had two sons. And the younger of them said to his father, 'Father, give me the share of property that is coming to me.' And he divided his property between them. Not many days later, the younger son gathered all he had and took a journey into a far country, and there he squandered his property in reckless living. And when he had spent everything, a severe famine arose in that country,

and he began to be in need. So he went and hired himself out to one of the citizens of that country, who sent him into his fields to feed pigs. And he was longing to be fed with the pods that the pigs ate, and no one gave him anything. But when he came to himself, he said, 'How many of my father's hired servants have more than enough bread, but I perish here with hunger! I will arise and go to my father, and I will say to him, "Father, I have sinned against heaven and before you. I am no longer worthy to be called your son. Treat me as one of your hired servants."' And he arose and came to his father. But while he was still a long way off, his father saw him and felt compassion, and ran and embraced him and kissed him. And the son said to him, 'Father, I have sinned against heaven and before you. I am no longer worthy to be called your son.' But the father said to his servants, 'Bring quickly the best robe, and put it on him, and put a ring on his hand, and shoes on his feet. And bring the fattened calf and kill it, and let us eat and celebrate. For this my son was dead, and is alive again; he was lost, and is found.' And they began to celebrate. Now his older son was in the field, and as he came and drew near to the house, he heard music and dancing. And he called one of the servants and asked what these things meant. And he said to him, 'Your brother has come, and your father has killed the fattened calf, because he has received him back safe and sound.' But he was angry and refused to go in. His father came out and entreated him, but he answered his father, 'Look, these many years I have served you, and I never disobeyed your command, yet you never gave me a young goat, that I might celebrate with my friends. But when this son of yours came, who has devoured your property with prostitutes, you killed the fattened calf for him!' And he said to him, 'Son, you are always with me, and all that is mine is yours. It was fitting to celebrate and be glad, for this your brother was dead, and is alive; he was lost, and is found.'" (Luke 15:11–32)

There are countless principles and applications that can be pulled from this passage, so please don't see this as even a close-to-complete treatment as I am after a few ideas that relate specifically to this book.

The first thing I'd like to discuss is what were the two sons after or what did they care about with respect to their father. For the younger brother, this is obvious as he just wanted his father's money, his portion of the inheritance, that he could go spend it on every pleasurable vice his heart could conceive of.

For the older brother, the motive takes a little more work to pull out. When the younger brother returns, this is the most joyous day of the father's life because his son, who was dead, has been returned to him alive. Yet the older brother did not see it this way, could not even conceive of viewing it through this lens. He was angry with his father for spending significant resources, which ultimately belonged to him, the older brother, as the father says to him, "All that I have is yours." You see, the older brother didn't really care about the father either, not to mention his own brother, his heart being identical to his younger brother, only really caring about the father's money, his portion of the inheritance.

These two brothers, these two sons, really had the same sinful heart and desire, which was one after wealth and power, above the love of each other and their own father. The differences between them was not found at the core of their hearts, which were virtually identical, but in the way that they expressed these sinful desires in their actions. The difference in this expression comes down to one key perspective, their view of "the law." By "the law," I am referring to the moral truths, principles, and rules that God has set forth directly and through human institutions for us to live by.

The younger brother sees these "laws" as the essence or embodiment of a "kill joy," that true life, meaning, worth, and value are found outside of the law, that I can obtain all that life has to offer by challenging the system, including the normal process for gaining my inheritance, the death of my father. The older brother sees the "law" and its perfect fulfillment as the means of achieving the sinful desires of his heart, that true life, meaning, worth, and value is found in my own self-righteousness and will help me attain the wealth and position that will grant me true fulfillment in life.

The truth is that life, value, worth, and meaning is not found in attaining your sinful, selfish desires outside the law or through the law; but truly it is found in relationship with the Father and likewise one another, the Greatest Commandment! Even though their lives and sins couldn't have manifested in more opposing ways, they both missed where real life was found. Even the younger brother, when he was lying in the mud, only thought to go back that he might live out his days as a servant with a full belly. Concerning the older brother, we are left with his story unfinished, the father inviting him to rejoice and be reconciled with himself and his brother, not knowing what he ultimately chooses…

One might wonder why Jesus, who is always purposeful, would end the story this way. Well, in context, this parable is the last of three related parables, including the parable of the Lost Sheep and the Lost Coin. These three parables begin, however, with the following verses:

> Now the tax collectors and sinners were all drawing near to hear him [Jesus]. And the Pharisees and the scribes grumbled, saying, "This man receives sinners and eats with them." So he [Jesus] told them this parable. (Luke 15:1–3)

You see, this parable was addressed to a group of "older brother" types, the scribes and Pharisees, who were passing judgment and trying to prevent the "younger brother" types of tax collectors and sinners from coming to Jesus and ultimately the Father. In actuality, the end of this parable is an invitation to this group of religious elites to come to the party, to rejoice with, have fellowship with, and receive the life and value found in the Father, which could only be achieved through His son, Jesus (John 14:6). It is the same offer he extends to each one of us! Will you join the party?

The Brotherhoodedness Spectrum

So far, we have seen that sin is a heart condition but one which can be expressed in very different ways. I call this difference of expression a characteristic or trait known as "brotherhoodedness." In my experience, each person lives on a spectrum that either leans toward being an "older brother" or "younger brother" not in the age sense but in the nature of how they view the world and likewise their sinful tendencies and its expressions.

Younger-brother types are typically a much more outwardly rebellious bunch. They either outrightly cross every line they can find or the more subtle and crafty ones see just how close they can get to the line without it costing them something. Their sins are usually expressed externally in very clear ways, on display for the world to see and know. These are the woman at the well, the woman caught in adultery, the tax collectors and sinners. The truth is that they often know they are sinful, willingly breaking God's law. The earthly consequences of their lifestyle usually catches up with them, leading to real brokenness and hopefully an openness to the gospel.

Older-brother types are typically much more inwardly rebellious. They steer clear of every potential line to cross and often make rules and laws that go above what God requires as a matter of personal pride. Their sins are usually hidden and concealed deep within their hearts, veiled in their external "righteousness." Truly, many of the Pharisees of Jesus's day knew and read the Scriptures, prayed, and gave to the synagogue with an intensity and fervor that would surpass even the most dedicated of Christians today yet were so sinful and far from God within that when He revealed Himself in the flesh, they called for and realized His death! These are the Pharisees, hypocrites, and white-washed tombs. The truth is they are often blind to their sins of pride, judgement, gossip, and self-righteousness. Their sins do not usually incur significant earthly consequences but are far more dangerous as left unchecked carry consequences over into eternity, a far worse fate.

As I am describing these personality types, I am sure that there are people coming into your mind. We all know people that embody these two very different mind-sets. We might even be one of them. There are some whose brotherhoodedness is less pronounced; but in my experience, most people lean to one side of this spectrum or the other. Interestingly enough, this quality is malleable in that it can change over time. Some people grow up as younger brothers without God and, after starting to follow Jesus, can embrace an older-brother mentality. Others are the reverse of that. There are still others who, in a church setting, act very much as an older brother; but outside of church, they are a younger brother to the core. Concerning actual birth order, I have noticed that actual firstborn children are more likely to be older-brother types and later born, younger brothers, but it is often also reversed.

To wrap up this concept of brotherhoodness, I thought it would be fun to list some well-known characters from history and pop culture that embody these two mind-sets.

> *Star Trek:* Captain Kirk (YB), Spock (OB)
> **New Testament:** Apostle Paul (OB), Apostle Peter (YB)
> **Marvel Cinematic Universe (before accords in Civil War):** Captain America (OB), Tony Stark (YB)
> *Star Wars:* C3PO (OB), R2D2 (YB)
> **Think up some more on you own...**

Approaches Considered

Coming full circle to my original investigation at the University of Minnesota all those years ago, we now see that much of why Jesus handled people differently was dependent on whether they were older brothers or younger brothers in nature. True, the core of their hearts are fundamentally the same, filled with sinful desires. Yet because of the way that they express them and view the world, they require different strategies and approaches in reaching them.

Jesus's approach. To those that are younger brothers, broken in their sinful ways, Jesus came alongside of them to show them grace and pull them up out of the muck and mire of their sin. He wasn't afraid of their sins and would routinely engage with them, being judged as a friend of tax collectors and sinners, often sharing meals with them. He would speak the truth but with an unrivaled grace and compassion, having called Himself the Great Physician to heal their spiritual sickness. To those that are older brother types, He would confront them head on in their sins. This was because, in their pride and self-righteousness, they couldn't even see the sinfulness of their own hearts. His goal was to pull them down off their judgmental perch and spiritual ivory towers that they might see they are wretched, poor, naked, and blind, being no better than the younger brothers they routinely condemn.

Typical church approach. Unfortunately within the church, I have often seen a different approach to that of Christ, much more akin to that of the mall preachers described earlier, but without quite the bite. Many times in church communities, we see the younger-brother types almost as a contagious disease. Their sins are usually on display for all to see and are the ones we talk about almost exclusively. We often ostracize them, causing them to feel guilt and shame, like second-class citizens of the Kingdom. Where Jesus reached down to pull them up out of their sin, we have a tendency to push them further down into it and, in some cases, right out of the door of our churches. In terms of the older-brother types, we often praise their perfection sometimes to the point where we might question whether they even need Jesus. We also usually don't address their internal sins, like pride, judgment, self-righteousness, and gossip, which are far more dangerous from an eternal perspective. Instead of helping them come down off their prideful perch, we often add fuel to the fire of their sin, with continuous praise and positive comparison to their "younger" counterparts.

You see, in the process of helping people become like Jesus and actively participating in their sanctification process, we must help them wrestle through their sin. If we are to do this effectively, we must not continue to be ignorant in our understanding of how sin affects each person in different ways, especially regarding brotherhoodedness!

My Own Attempts

Over the past twenty years of experimenting in discipleship, identifying the unique ways in which sin affects each of us and learning to address it more like Jesus, has been probably the single most important tool I have discovered. Ask any parent with more than one child and they will tell you they can't teach, encourage, or correct them all in the same way and those that do, do so at their own peril. In much the same way, we disciple people in a one-size-fits-all approach at our own peril, not to mention theirs.

If you find yourself discipling a younger brother, here are few approaches I have found helpful and freeing truths to share:

> ➤ Help them understand that God's law and most rules do not exist to keep them from happiness but are there to protect them, that although many of these off-limit things can bring temporary pleasure, they also produce a toxic venom that slowly takes your life and leaves you void of all happiness.

> ➤ That everyone is a sinner and that, in those regards, you are no different than others, that many of the people, especially within the church, that seem to have it all together and might hold this in front of your face are often just as sinful as you are. The only difference is that their sins look very different. In this sense, you should not feel inferior to them and instead should extend grace and truth, knowing that you are both in the same proverbial boat.

> That although you may feel unworthy, and the truth is you are, that God's love and grace abounds. For where sin did abound, grace did truly abound much more in Jesus. You are not outside God's forgiveness and Kingdom; for Jesus came to seek and save that which was lost, you!

> To understand that their sins often come along with many unfortunate consequences in this life and that, although sometimes God saves us from them, often it is His grace that we experience these consequences, typically being the best teacher of younger brothers.

> This might seem odd, but I also tell them that I know they are likely going to sin in some outwardly, rotten ways but that this doesn't put them outside God's grace and love and my own concern and affection—that God is not afraid of their sin and neither am I, that I am there with them, like Jesus was with Peter, through the countless boneheaded moments, and that, like Peter, God still has something significant for them to do. They are not disqualified as Pastor Peter denied even knowing Jesus and within weeks was restored and preached three thousand people into the Kingdom.

If you find yourself discipling an older brother, here are few approaches I have found helpful and freeing truths to share:

> If you spend much time with an older brother, you will generally notice subtle attitudes of judgement and superiority coloring much of what they say and their general attitudes. Try and draw these conversations back to places of Christ-centered grace and mercy and Jesus's thoughts and approaches in these situations. Challenge them to pray for or encourage and support those that they pass judgement toward or look down on. What are you doing for your brother or sister? Invite them to the party!

> Go over as many passages as you can where Jesus addresses the older brother attitude and heart. Ask them how they see these verses playing out in the church and their own

lives. Let the truth of God's Word and the Spirit continually reveal the dark hidden places in their hearts, ultimately bringing deliverance and freedom that pride has kept at bay. In my experience, this process usually takes at least a year or two; and many times I have had a church kid come to me without any prompting after a year or more of occasionally reflecting on these ideas and passages with both excitement and brokenness, telling me that they finally see their sin and need for God's grace.

➢ Go over the Parable of the Prodigal Son and ask them to self-identify their brotherhoodedness. Help them understand that the heart of the older and younger brothers are the same and that actually the heart of the older brother is the more dangerous of the two because it more often leads to eternal consequences.

➢ If you are yourself an older brother, share your experiences of how God has dealt with you in this area and brought freedom to you. As an older brother myself, I have found this to be the single most effective method.

➢ If you are dealing with older brothers that are so hardened that they simply refuse to see the destruction that their pride and judgement are having on themselves and those around them, you may need to confront them in direct and challenging ways. You are not passing judgment here but sternly warning them of where this path will lead. In my experience, this approach is not a common one I have had to employ, nor is it one I enjoy using. But when all else has failed, like Jesus, it is the only compassionate thing to do. The stakes are just too high to do anything else!

Hopefully these thoughts will help you both in your own personal introspection as you become a disciple of Jesus and in encouraging the many different types of people He will bring across your path. May God by His grace also give you additional wisdom and insight into handling the complex and sinful tendencies of the human heart.

In Summary

Truly one of my biggest concerns, maybe even fears, over the years of serving in ministry is the thought that I and many in the church have been producing Pharisees instead of disciples of Jesus. In the best of cases, this means prideful, judgmental Christians; in the worst of cases, it means people who think that they are righteous but are actually outside of Christ and likewise salvation. This point cannot be overstated. Literally, people's souls are on the line. That is not to say, as I laid out in the chapter "A Work of Grace" that it is our job to fix all older brothers as even Jesus did not succeed in this task. **At the same time, we cannot and must not be naive to the deceitfulness and cunning of sin in all its varied and sinister forms!** In becoming more like Jesus, both ourselves and supporting others in that process, we must see sin clearly as an inward condition of our hearts. We must be wise, by God's grace, to the motives and intentions of hearts, irrespective of actions, especially seemingly godly ones. I wish it was simpler. God, I wish it was simpler… The heart of the matter is that it's the heart that matters and much of the heart is hidden. As I am writing this, I am praying that God gives us insight into helping to address with both grace and truth any selfish motives within our own hearts and the hearts of those God has called us to walk beside that we all might become a little more like Jesus!

Personal Challenge

> ➤ Do you associate more with the heart and attitude of an older brother or a younger brother? Has this attitude changed throughout your life?
> ➤ Think about people in your life that are close to you. Can you see older brother or younger brother tendencies in them?
> ➤ How do you normally treat older-brother types? Has this chapter affected your approach going forward and if so, how?

> ➤ How do you normally treat younger-brother types? Has this chapter affected your approach going forward and if so, how?
> ➤ How can you apply these ideas to both your own disciple-ship and your discipling of others?

Tools of the Trade

Look carefully then how you walk, not as unwise but as wise, making the best use of the time, because the days are evil. (Ephesians 5:15–16)

I love to think! There are times when I can get lost in thought for hours, literally even days at a time. I believe this to very likely be some type of condition, which I have come to refer to as "hyper-analytical." This "condition" is characterized by the need for everything I perceive and everything I encounter to be explainable and fit neatly within the framework of how I understand the world around me or else an ensuing war rages within as I try to beat the nonconforming thought or experience into submitting to my understanding. This trait was almost certainly exacerbated by the fact that my schooling and much of my professional life has been as an engineer, where I literally was paid large sums of money to analyze the heights of complexity for hours on end every single day.

One important problem, not engineering related, that I have been giving brain cycles to for well over fifteen years has been, "How to effectively live out the biblical mandate of relational discipleship in a culture that is diametrically opposed to it?" I am regularly burdened by thoughts like... "I am called to train and teach others by doing life with them..." "To regularly use my gifts and talents for the building up of the saints..." "To love my brethren with the same love Jesus has demonstrated toward me..."

Yet trying to plan a short meeting with just one other person is often a complicated series of proposed dates and times usually resulting in a date at least one, often two or more weeks out, and half of those get rescheduled due to other unforeseen conflicts. You see the problem with this? To help you get a better flavor of what is going on in my mind, here is some open access to how my brain engages with problems like this...

"I am called to consider others before myself, to be servant of all, to lose my life that I might gain His. Yet I live in a society that teaches me it is all about, well, me—my time, my preferences, my benefit, or, as Bon Jovi put it best, "It's my life!"

I am called to disciple those around me, but I live in a society where we often outsource some of our most important responsibilities to others, especially when it comes to spiritual matters.

I am called to a discipleship process that likely requires years of dedication, sacrifice, and investment, but I live in a society that is built on instant gratification, a microwave generation, who gets upset if it takes a few extra seconds for a website to load on their smart phone.

I am called to share meaningful things with others, to sing songs, hymns, and spiritual songs to one another yet live in a society that discourages and fails to equip people to discuss weighty subjects like philosophy, politics, and theology, especially in healthy ways.

We are supposed to live in close community, but many live in sprawling suburbs that remove them from their family and friends. We don't know the people in our communities because we can't walk anywhere, entering and exiting our homes often without encountering a soul.

We can name numerous people that we've been meaning to see, and we remind ourselves every time we randomly cross their path that a meeting is on the horizon but only perpetually so... Yet as a disciple, we are called to live in a vibrant faith community, regularly using our gifts and talents to encourage and strengthen those around us.

As you can see, there is a lot to overcome in trying to live out the biblical mandate and model we have been discussing. To live this way is synonymous with a call to live counterculturally, to swim upstream, to cut against the grain, or any other such cliché you can think of.

After fifteen years of pondering this problem, I still have not found a satisfactory solution, at least not good enough for my liking. That said, in this chapter, I hope to provide you with some of the most effective strat-

egies I have discovered and developed for trying to live out this lifestyle of disciple making in our current culture. And with that, I hope you enjoy!

Congratulations! You have made it through most of the concepts required to start answering God's call as a disciple maker. As advertised, this chapter is dedicated to a few additional tips or "tools of the trade" that I have discovered during my own personal journey in answering this call. There are obviously many more, which the Lord will teach you as you engage in this process, but it is my hope and prayer that the short list here helps you avoid some of the pitfalls and frustrations that I and countless others have faced in this countercultural endeavor.

Intentionality

I believe being intentional or intentionality is the single most important "practical tip" for anyone desiring to engage in making disciples. Being intentional about discipleship is at its core a state of heart and mind or an ethos where you are consistently purposeful with your time, treasure, and talent for the edification of others.

So what does this look like? It means that as you converse with, work with, travel with, and generally do life with others, you are constantly and actively considering how, by God's grace, you can help them become more like Jesus. You are tirelessly on the lookout for "discipling opportunities" and purposefully place yourself in situations where discipleship can take place. Just look at how intentional Jesus was with His disciples, effectively using every moment and situation to train them to maturity. Their three years of doing life together was a transformational course in becoming like Him because Jesus was intentional with their time together, embracing and utilizing every moment they had. If you can adopt this mind-set, attitude, and ethos, it will not only change your life but that of those around you!

Finding Time

The problem of "finding time" is especially difficult in our American culture. Just as it is true that God is good all the time, so too we are "busy" all the time! We have seen throughout this discussion that effective discipleship requires real relationships, doing life together; and that requires time, time that no one believes they have.

The truth is our American culture stands in complete opposition to this relational characteristic of the Christian life and seems to progressively be getting worse. With the advent of social media and limitless options for entertainment and recreation, genuine relationships are often sacrificed on the altar of personal pleasure. Meaningful, deep, committed relationships continue to be the marginalized exception and not the prevailing rule, even within the church.

I am not here trying to pass blame or judgment for these failings as we have literally everything working against us in this effort. If I dare say, it seems likely that this is a coordinated assault by the Devil, deceiving us with an endless array of passing substitutes for what our hearts truly long for. All I am wanting to do here is draw attention to depths of these issues, which are so prevalent and engrained in our culture, they can at times seem normal. They are not. Yet although the hurdle to find time is a difficult one, I know from experience it is possible. It just requires a little creativity. The following list contains a few practical tips and techniques I have found to battle the scheduling nightmares caused by seemingly endless busyness.

> ➤ **Everyone needs to eat:** Thankfully we all need to take time out of our day to pause from activity and eat, unless you're into that whole working lunch thing. Since eating doesn't usually require much focus or thought, unless you are me trying to use chopsticks, this a perfect activity to leverage for discipleship. I have personally had more epic times of laughter, encouragement, and instruction over meals or some fine beverage than any other activity. If someone says they don't have time, ask them if they eat (they do) and

would be willing to do that together. If all else fails, tell them you'll pay...

➢ **Scheduling and planning:** I have found if you expect spontaneous or spur of the moment plans to come together regularly, you will often be disappointed. It is quite unlikely that your schedule aligns with a time when the person or people in question are both motivated and able to meet. To combat this, I have found that if you look one to two weeks out, you can usually find a mutually available time. Unfortunately, this strategy goes against most people's natural tendencies; but if you want to meet with someone consistently, I know of no other way.

➢ **Along for the ride:** Often we don't have the time within our own schedules to dedicate toward discipleship, or at least not enough. One creative and efficient way to get around this is to turn ordinary tasks into discipleship opportunities. You see, engaging in discipleship does not have to be a dedicated activity, and often it can be more effective if you are incorporating it into some other activity. It is during these typically mundane moments where you can model, instruct, and give people opportunities to grow and become like Jesus in the regular routines of life. As an example, you can turn tandem, activities like running errands, volunteering somewhere, cooking a meal, working out, or just about any other thing you would normally do solo. This often provides not only great opportunities to converse and connect; but just like Jesus with His disciples, unplanned teaching and training opportunities often present themselves. So whatever you are doing, bring others along for the ride, literally. Or you can always tag along for the ride with them.

These are just a smattering of strategies for finding time in our fast-paced and over-obligated culture. I encourage you to creatively and prayerfully find a few of your own strategies. Although it might be challenging, you can find or make the time! Or better yet, make more efficient use of time planned for other things!

Catalyzing Events

Another important tool that is relatively simple is what I refer to as a "catalyzing event." For the unfamiliar, a catalyst is something that greatly speeds up a process or reaction, in this case, making disciples. I have discovered over the years that the only thing needed to successfully "kick-start" the discipleship process is spending more than twenty-four consecutive hours together. Almost without regard to the activity you are doing, spending at least a full day together with someone has an almost miraculous way of creating connection and breaking down barriers.

I have personally experienced countless trips, retreats, camps, or other extended activities that resulted in the formation of new meaningful friendships. If you believe that the discipleship process really is the messy relational enterprise described in this book, then finding effective and efficient ways to connect with others is unquestionably essential. I would argue this approach is almost certainly the best. An additional benefit is that the relational depth gained during such activities makes every future activity, no matter the duration, much more meaningful being able to draw on the currency of shared experiences and trust. The takeaway here is simple. **If you want to engage in discipleship, one of the single best things you can do to supercharge the process is go spend twenty-four hours together, better yet two to three days or even more!**

One Size Does Not Fit All

Every person is unique. Each of us has different gifts, passions, struggles, and learning styles. Despite this, many have endeavored to build one-size-fits-all comprehensive discipleship curriculums and programs. These curriculums function much like getting a college degree, where you have a fixed set of course requirements and information to learn, which after completing, you will have "graduated."

Obviously, this streamlined approach is tempting as it enables us to bring everyone through the exact same content and declare success when they have demonstrated the ability to accurately recite the information in question. Now I believe that these curriculums are often well intentioned and can indeed support spiritual growth; but as we have discussed, they have some fundamental flaws. It is impossible for them, on their own, to produce mature disciples whose lives have been transformed in faith, truth, and love, especially when they make no accounting for any of the uniqueness that each of us was created with.

To be clear, I am not saying that there aren't core principles and training that can be given to everyone in the same way, just that I don't think it is possible to make a comprehensive, universal "discipleship degree." Anyone who has helped raise or teach children knows this to be true. Parents the world over have tried the same parenting style or techniques on different children, only to realize that what worked for one often has the opposite effect on another. Even Jesus himself engaged with people differently depending on who they were as we discussed at length in the last chapter.

The truth is that a "one-size-fits-all" approach just doesn't work for all. Instead, the application and, in some cases, the content needs to be unique based again on the struggles, passions, gifts, and learning style of each person. It means that to be effective in discipleship, you can't just teach canned content. Instead, you must engage in the labor-intensive process of asking good questions and observing the life of the one you are discipling, much as the way a parent is aware of the spiritual, mental, and emotional state of their children. To effectively disciple others, you must be aware of how God has made them and what's going on in their life and adjust your training accordingly.

God's Training Plan

The idea here is a simple one. **God has a perpetual training plan for each one of us that is unique to who we are, what we need, and are called to do.**

Lest we forget, it is God who ultimately sets the curriculum for our life and those we disciple. For some of us, it is easy to get focused on stringent, formalized training plans for others, which again are not necessarily bad but should never replace or usurp God's training plan for us. Never forget we have His Spirit living inside of us, who leads us and illuminates God's truth to our minds and hearts moment by moment and day by day, teaching and training us continually from the inside out.

Truthfully, most of the time, I don't know what someone else needs because their future, their inner struggles, and their true passions are often veiled from my sight, often even theirs. The good news is I know someone who perceives all and has already developed a training plan for their life, a plan of which I am privileged to take part in.

So what does this mean practically? In my experience, it has driven me to my knees, spending countless hours discerning what God is trying to teach each person I meet with and for the grace to get onboard, being a part of and reinforcing His lessons. Specifically, give the following two principles a try:

> **Ask them what God has been teaching them or what they have been wrestling with.** Inevitably this question leads to great discussion and often real transformation as it usually reflects the work that the Lord is currently doing in their life. It also helps them to reflect on and be aware that God is actively working in them and how important it is to be aware of and sensitive to this.

> **Ask God what He is wanting to teach and encourage them with.** Before meeting with someone, I almost always pray and ask the Lord for guidance in our time together. This can be as simple as a few minutes on the drive over. Usually I sense the Lord put a topic, thought, or activity on my heart. It has been one of the most encouraging things over the years to see how consistently and profoundly what the Lord puts on my heart is exactly what that person needed. Go figure.

If you truly want to be effective in transformational discipleship, stop trying in your own wisdom to design the perfect training plan for another and instead play your small part in God's training plan for their life!

Ask Lots of Questions

So often people believe that discipleship is just about having and giving all the answers. The following thought may surprise you; but even if you had all the answers, simply giving the perfect answer for every question is not the best way to disciple someone. How do we know this? Well, Jesus was the best disciple maker to ever live, literally the gold standard, having basically all of the answers (except one, the day and hour), and it was far from His approach.

During His recorded ministry, Jesus asked 307 questions, was asked 183 questions, of which He only answered 3. We usually think of Jesus as the guy with all the answers; and even though that is true (being literally the embodiment of truth, the Word made flesh), just blurting out those answers wasn't how He rolled. Jesus instead was usually about asking questions, and there are several reasons why this approach is important to spiritual development. The following are just a few:

> **Makes them think:** Something important happens when we ask people to think through something. They are forced to wrestle with the idea and internalize it. They are required to be an active participant in uncovering truth as opposed to a passive listener that is likely to forget or never truly understand what is being said in the first place. Challenge people to think critically and actively engage with truth by asking great questions!

> **They already have the answer:** Often times, people already have the answer to their questions buried within or can easily find it using their God-given intellect. The problem is that they usually aren't asking the right question to begin

124

with or in the right way or, in some cases, are just plain lazy. You can help lead people to discover the right answer, which they often already have within, by simply helping them ask the right questions.

> **Builds their confidence:** When you give people the answers to every question they have, it builds confidence and reliance, although not on themselves and God but on you! In the process of spiritual growth and development, you want to build their confidence in God and their own God-given abilities. By asking questions where they arrive at the answer themselves, you are not only giving them truth but also fostering a belief that they can arrive at the truth without you. If you want to build mature disciples, developing this confidence is a necessity and requires that you don't spoon-feed them every answer. Their ability to discern truth is often as important to foster as the specific truths you are sharing with them.

Unfortunately, most teaching in our churches today is an extremely refined and spoon-fed meal to congregants. There is definitely a time and place for this, and God has given people gifts within the Body for this kind of ministry. This must not, however, be the only thing in their spiritual diets. In some ways, continuous feeding of this type can actually hinder spiritual growth by producing a dependence on others for all of your spiritual answers. In building mature disciples, we are to work ourselves out of a job of being their source of answers. We need to be like Jesus and help them learn to discover truth on their own, in many cases by simply by asking great questions!

I wish I had time and space to unpack the countless strategies and approaches for asking good questions to facilitate mental and spiritual growth. Unfortunately, that could be an entire book in itself. If this topic interests you, I would recommend reading or watching any decent resources you can find on the Socratic method and study the questions that Jesus asked others. That said, a sample of interesting questions you can ask people to support their spiritual growth and development are:

> **Fundamental definitions of well known but not well understood terms:** What is sin? What is faith? What is grace? Or as Foreigner said, "I want to know what love is." When they give simple "Sunday school answers," challenge their thinking with follow-up and clarifying questions. For example, if they say sin is a bunch of wrong actions, ask them if you can sin without doing anything and show them a corresponding passage or just have them read it and compare it to their initial answer. Or ask them if the biblical definition of love differs from our cultural definition, in what ways and why? How does that difference impact our society, how we read the Bible, and how we understand God's love? I think you get the idea.

> **Discerning motive and purpose behind cultural norms:** Why do we do that? Why do we go to church on Sundays? Why do we have elders in our church? Why do we go on mission trips? Why do we lay hands on people? And a whole host of other things that we do all the time but probably don't know why other than that's what we do...

> **Looking beyond the words:** In any biblical passage, we can ask, "Why is the author saying what they are saying?" What is the core idea they are trying to get across or behavior they are trying to influence?

> **Ask introspective questions:** What has God called you to do with your life? To be? Is there a deeper issue or cause behind the sins and things you struggle with? What do you believe about how God sees you or what He thinks about you? Who are you to God? How do you primarily see God? Father, friend, lord, savior, judge, teacher, comforter, brother, etc.?

This is just a smattering of a whole host of questions you can be asking those you are discipling. What is even more powerful than these initial questions is good follow-up questions where you force them to be more logically consistent, clear, and precise with their answers. Call into question contradictions or overly ambiguous points, forcing them to wrestle and squirm a little as they search for the truth! You can even practice these techniques to discover truth on your own by answering your own well-formed questions. Good questions in this case are indeed the answer!

Do Something Fun

Why so serious? Don't make everything about overly spiritual activities or deep theological truths, you "older brother" you. Sometimes the best way to connect and encourage open dialogue and relationships is just to go have some fun together. Maybe go to a sporting event or movie? Maybe play a board game or go on a camping trip? Not a lot more here to say other than don't be so darn serious all the time. God gave us laughter for a reason. Just go have some fun together from time to time!

Personal Challenge

- ➤ Spend the next few days focusing on being intentional with people around you in the normal course of life as it relates to discipleship.
- ➤ Spend some time practicing asking good questions to either yourself or others.
- ➤ Select one or more practical tools of the trade from above and come up with a plan to try it out in the coming weeks.
- ➤ Come up with your own creative, outside-the-box way to engage in discipleship and try it out in the weeks to come.

Discipleship Here, There, and Everywhere!

> Now there are varieties of gifts, but the same Spirit; and there are varieties of service, but the same Lord; and there are varieties of activities, but it is the same God who empowers them all in everyone. To each is given the manifestation of the Spirit for the common good. (1 Corinthians 12:4–7)

As an engineer, I have assisted in the design and development of numerous things like unmanned spy planes, signal processing microcontrollers, cellular remote monitoring systems, and optically controlled electronic slide guitars, just to name a few. Although significant creativity is involved, in the end, every part of the design needs to follow a precise process, being tightly controlled and structured! It is this very structured way of thinking and working for which I am naturally wired, no pun intended. Knowing that's how I operate, one of the things that has challenged and surprised me over the years is how seemingly spontaneous and outside the normative boundaries of traditional church and life the process of making disciples has been.

People often ask me if I have a "program" for what I do or bring others through? I do not.

They ask me how I find people to disciple. I tell them Jesus brings them.

They ask me how I start with people. I tell them I just bite the awkward bullet and go for it.

As an example, just a few weeks back, I was having dinner with a friend, and we ran into a former coworker of his and got to talking a little. While we were talking, I sensed that little nudge of the Spirit I have come to know and embrace over the years; and five minutes later, I asked my friend's coworker if they would like to meet up and chat sometime. Three weeks later, we met for coffee, and the Lord provided a chance for me to speak some encouraging and few challenging words into their life for well over two hours.

To be clear, I am not saying I haven't found significant value within well-structured church services, programs, and activities, quite the opposite, and it is to these that I naturally gravitate. The Lord has used these programs and activities in profound ways, and they have also served as a launching point to connect me with others for follow-up activities. That said, I want to challenge your thinking as the Lord has challenged mine. I humbly ask you to think outside the box of the bread-and-butter church services, programs, and activities. How can you use them as a launching point to engage with people in a deeper way?

You see, no matter how hard we try, it is impossible, not to mention exhausting, to construct formal church programs and events to meet every need and engage every person where they are at. I praise God we don't even need to try but that, by His Spirit, He is continually knitting us together to be His hands and feet one to another, if we would only be open to it, on the lookout for it, and at the ready to embrace it!

To summarize these musings, as a very structural and logical thinker trying to follow Jesus, I have been forced to embrace what often appears to me as random and unstructured leadings of His Spirit. The truth, however, is that they are not random or unstructured. They just don't fit into my own conception of how things should be ordered. You see, the Lord isn't building some rigid structure, organization, or professional program; He is organizing a vibrant, dynamic, living organism, His own Body here on earth! This Body, much like our own, is composed of countless complex connections and interactions. As Paul encouraged us in our ministry to each other that it should embody the pattern of every relational joint or connection supplying the love and life of God, one to another.

It is my prayer for you, as well as myself, that we can continue to be open to fulfilling this Great Commission through not only the programs, services, and activities of our local Church but, like Jesus who ministered at a moment's notice, live as ready, noble vessels, in season and out, to help people embrace and embody Him!

During His three years of earthly ministry, Jesus did not have a one-size-fits-all approach to the people He reached. Instead, He brought life-changing transformation to countless individuals in just about every type of setting with a variety of methods. Whether teaching from a boat or casting demons out on a hillside or having a meal with tax collectors and sinners, His ministry was anything but typical and always dynamic! As His disciples, does our ministry embody this symphony of expression, or is it pretty one note?

Throughout most of this book, we have discussed discipleship through the lens of a long-term investment of a more mature Christ follower into the life of a less mature one. This was done purposefully to help simplify the discussion, as it is arguably the clearest form or picture of discipleship, being the model that Jesus used in developing the Twelve. It is not the only model or method though. Just as Jesus brought transformation to countless others outside the Twelve, we too should embrace all the different avenues that the Lord has provided for us to help make disciples. To this end, the final chapter is devoted to exploring the many varied ways you can, by God's grace, help others become more like Jesus! Get ready to partake in a sampling or taste test of the many flavors of discipleship ministry!

Pauls and Timothies and Barnabi, Oh My!

In our calling to both become and make disciples, the Lord has set in place three primary relational roles to foster this process, each contributing in its own way. Throughout this book, we have focused primarily on one of these, as stated earlier, but all three are indeed critical components of spiritual health and growth. Thankfully, no matter what the relational role, essentially all of the principles outlined in this book still apply. To help clarify these three different relationships, we will now unpack them using the life of the apostle Paul as an example.

> **Paul to Timothy:** Paul was called by God to come alongside a young man named Timothy to teach, train, and invest his very life into this blossoming missionary and pastor. Paul was a more mature believer, who saw within Timothy a God-given potential and was committed to not letting it go to waste. He not only helped Timothy become a mature and effective follower of Jesus, but He also gained a dear spiritual son and friend in the process. This is the type of relationship we have focused on throughout this book. God is calling each of us to be a Paul to someone!

> **Timothy to Paul:** Timothy was a young man, raised in a Christian home with a calling from God on his life, but he needed a Paul to show him the way. He needed someone to model what it meant to be a mature follower of Jesus, especially in the context of pastoring and planting churches. Not only did he gain this example in Paul but also a dear spiritual father. God is calling each of us to have a Paul in our life!

> **Paul and Barnabas:** Barnabas, whose name means son of encouragement, was a peer of Paul and co-laborer in the Kingdom. God sent them out together, to be friends in this life who would stand by each other, encouraging and rejoicing with one another through the valleys and mountaintops of life. Within these peer relationships, many of the same discipleship principles we have outlined apply in similar ways. God is calling each of us to both have and be a Barnabas!

Again, God uses every one of these relational models to help us become mature disciples, each being absolutely critical, having its unique place and role.

In life, we all need Pauls, people to help train and equip us to fulfill God's call on our life and grow into mature disciples of Jesus.

In life, we all need Timothies, people who we can come alongside and help become mature disciples of Jesus and, in the process, become more like Jesus ourselves.

In life, we all need Barnabi, people that walk through life with us, encouraging us and us them, working together as co-laborers as we become more like Jesus.

To delve deeper into these relational models, I encourage you to study the book of Acts with Paul and friends, the Gospels with Jesus and His Twelve, and the "pastoral letters or epistles" of first and second Timothy and Titus. That said, before we move on from this discussion, here are a couple practical points of interest:

> These relationships often evolve over time. Specifically, those whom you see as a Timothy will hopefully someday become a Barnabas to you.

> When it comes to having a Paul in your life, I often hear people say that this is something you should seek out. There is nothing wrong with seeking someone out, but Jesus's model had the "Paul" seek out the "Timothy." This is because it is the Paul who sees the potential in the Timothy, which the Timothy usually can't see within themselves.

Prayerful Consideration. For those that love the action steps and application, it doesn't get more real than this. I encourage you to make a consistent habit of praying for the Lord's guidance concerning these three questions:

> Is God calling you to be a Paul to someone and if so, who?
> Is God calling you to have a Paul in your life and if so, who?
> Is God calling you to do life with a Barnabi and if so, who?

For the literalists, you don't need to limit yourself to only one of each as it is expected that you have several of these relationships in your life. Additionally, these relationships might already exist, but God is calling you to be more intentional and make a greater investment based on the biblical principles we have discussed. My prayer here is that everyone reading this book would, by God's grace, have people above them to guide them, people around them that encourage them, and the joy of guiding others, that we would all embrace the fullness of our God-given privilege to be a part of God's Great Commission to make disciples, whether Pauls, Timothies, or Barnabi, oh my!

Head, Shoulders, Knees, and Toes

As we discussed briefly in the chapter on making disciples by God's grace, although we are all laborers with the same end goal in mind, not all of us play the same role in the process. Each of us is created by God to be a unique and indispensable part in the Body of Christ, His church. In this section, we will explore this clear New Testament concept as it is only through each of us embracing our God-given role that His church will thrive!

> Now there are varieties of gifts, but the same Spirit; and there are varieties of service, but the same Lord; and there are varieties of activities, but it is the same God who empowers them all in everyone. **To each is given the manifestation of the Spirit for the common good.** (Paul, 1 Corinthians 12:4–7)

Here we see that God, by His Spirit, gives unique and varied gifts unto His people for the common good. In his letter to the Romans, Paul further expands on this concept, saying:

> For as in one body we have many members, and the members do not all have the same function, so we, though many, are one body in Christ, and individually members one of another. Having gifts that differ according to the grace given to us, let us use them: if prophecy, in proportion to

our faith; if service, in our serving; the one who teaches, in his teaching; the one who exhorts, in his exhortation; the one who contributes, in generosity; the one who leads, with zeal; the one who does acts of mercy, with cheerfulness. (Paul, Romans 12:4–8)

We see here that it is through using these God-given gifts that we help those around us become more like Jesus. No matter what the relationship, whether as Pauls, Timothies, or Barnabi, we need to recognize the unique gifts and callings that God has blessed us with and use them for the common good. I encourage you to reflect on the gifts, talents, and resources that God has equipped you with. How has He positioned you in His Body of which He is the head and we are the shoulders, knees, toes, and appendix?

Finally, the following passage I think summarizes well how God desires us to live together as His Body:

Rather, speaking the truth in love, we are to grow up in every way into him who is the head, into Christ, from whom the whole body, joined and held together by every joint with which it is equipped, when each part is working properly, makes the body grow so that it builds itself up in love. (Paul, Ephesians 4:15–16)

This is an awesome image of what the Body of Christ looks like when it is healthy and vibrant, with each part playing its role, working in its proper order. Hands are not trying to be ears and eyes are not trying to be knees. Each part knows its place and has embraced it, causing the body to grow and build itself up in love until the church, His Body, is made whole, infused with and a vessel of His abundant life. It is my prayer that you discern your part and, by God's grace, use your gifts and talents in all your relationships for the spiritual growth and development of those around you!

A Moment, a Season, a Lifetime

In both reading the New Testament and in my personal experience, discipleship relationships typically come in one of three flavors regarding their duration. Specifically, some are for a moment, some are for a season, and some are for a lifetime!

As someone who thrives on close long-term relationships, this was at times a hard lesson for me to learn and embrace as I only desired the "lifetime version." What I ended up discovering is that lifetime relationships are often the most rare and momentary encouragement the most frequent, much to my dismay. In this section, we will explore how the Lord works in the relational disciple making process over time.

For a moment. During His ministry, there were numerous times where Jesus encountered people that He brought life and healing to. Jesus was filled with compassion, engaging with strangers at their point of need. The woman at the well, the demoniac, the woman caught in adultery, blind Bartimaeus and many more, all had short but significant encounters with Jesus. If we are open to it, the Lord wants to use our lives to draw others unto Him even if those interactions are momentary and fleeting.

Whether you meet someone sitting next to you on a plane ride, serving you at a restaurant, driving you in a taxi or Uber, or at a retreat, there are countless opportunities to minister to others. It could be an encouraging word, wisdom for a situation, sharing of an experience, praying with them, or simply just taking a genuine interest in their life. In this moment-based ministry, these relationships typically don't last longer than a few minutes, hours, or days but, as was the case with Jesus, can be significant enough to shape the course and trajectory of their lives. Be on the lookout for God-appointed discipleship moments!

For a season. During His ministry, the Lord brought the apostle Paul to many different cities to preach the gospel and establish thriving churches. In some cases, he would stay there for a year or more helping to get things firmly established. God often calls us to "seasons" of life, which could be for months, years, or even decades and are often marked by the job, social circles, or physical location where we live. During these seasons, Jesus will often bring people into our life to disciple for a significant portion or the entire duration of that season.

In my experience, these are usually some of the most impactful opportunities that we have as the extended time window offers greater depth of relationship and ultimately transformation. Yet just as actual seasons change, so do "seasons" in our life. When these life seasons shift, so often do these relationships which makes these some of the most challenging to have. Most of the time, we wish that these relationships could continue as they are forever, but it often isn't possible no matter how hard we try. Take for example Paul when he was called to leave some "seasonal friends."

> Therefore, be alert, remembering that for three years I did not cease night or day to admonish everyone with tears... And when he (Paul) had said these things, he knelt down and prayed with them all. And there was much weeping on the part of all; they embraced Paul and kissed him, being sorrowful most of all because of the word he had spoken, that they would not see his face again. And they accompanied him to the ship. (Paul to the church at Ephesus, Acts 20:31, 36–38)

As sad and difficult as these occasions might be, we must maintain a good perspective. Firstly, in calling both parties to different things, we should rejoice in the work that God will continue to do and the new lives we will get to encourage in the next season. Additionally and most importantly, these relationships never truly end as we literally have all of eternity to be with each other. This is our hope in Jesus! So embrace your season of life and transition with godly perspective when the Lord calls you to the next one!

For a lifetime. These types of relationships are typically rare, and you may only have a handful of them in your lifetime outside your immediate family. I believe it is God's grace that, amid all the momentary and seasonal relationships, He also provides a few consistent threads through it all. These people are truly gifts of God in your life, and I encourage you to cherish them as such as they are rare and precious gifts indeed!

An example of one such relationship, again with the apostle Paul, was his spiritual son Timothy, who stood by the side of his spiritual father faithfully through all life's challenges. Even though separated by significant time and distance during their lives, Timothy and Paul were God-given gifts to each other personally and in the establishment of God's Kingdom. Just read what the apostle Paul says about his spiritual son:

> I [Paul] hope in the Lord Jesus to send Timothy to you soon, so that I too may be cheered by news of you. For I have no one like him, who will be genuinely concerned for your welfare. For they all seek their own interests, not those of Jesus Christ. But you know Timothy's proven worth, how as a son with a father he has served with me in the gospel. I hope therefore to send him just as soon as I see how it will go with me, and I trust in the Lord that shortly I myself will come also. (Paul, Philippians 2:19–24)

As you walk through life, keep your eyes open for lifetime relationships, which often have their genesis as seasonal ones! Treat these as precious and things to always be cherished and nourished as God often uses these as spiritual bedrock to help stabilize and anchor you throughout the shifting times and seasons of life.

So whether momentary, seasonal, or lifelong, embrace the relationships and opportunities to love, encourage, and strengthen everyone Jesus brings along your path!

Bringing It All Together

Now for the grand finale where we bring together all the concepts of this book in one harmonious symphony!

There is one Problem that is the source of all the unfathomable wickedness in the world today, being sin, that has bound us to a hopeless fate of both physical and spiritual death.

Thanks be to God that He, through Jesus, provided a complete solution becoming God's wisdom and also our righteous, sanctification, and redemption.

God has also provided for us a truly awesome privilege in giving us a Great Commission whereby we are called to help people experience this purchased salvation through the process of making disciples of Jesus at an exponential rate to save the world.

These disciples of Jesus are not just moral or religious people but abide in God's Word, love others as Jesus has loved them, trust God with their lives, and engage in the process of making more disciples of Jesus, all stemming from a sincere and deep love for God.

We are not called to engage in this discipleship process alone; but as obedient co-laborers with God Himself, we must trust and rely on His strength to do a miracle in the hearts and minds of those that He has called us to disciple.

This call of making disciples is not optional; and though you might be unsure or timid, God's grace is sufficient. There are people all around you waiting to experience the Jesus in you.

This commission is a Jesus empowered, messy, relational enterprise by where we both model and provide opportunities for people to become like Jesus in mind, love, and faith.

Even though this process is antithetical to our cultural norms, through creative strategies and speaking to the needs of each individual, both older and younger brothers, we can overcome these hurdles.

Finally, whether as Pauls, Timothies, or Barnabi, for moments, seasons, or a lifetime, as shoulders, knees, or toes, we are called to engage people in becoming more like Jesus, here, there, and everywhere!

Opportunities Abound

Not sure if you remember; but all the way back in the intro-duction, I asked you to dream a little... I wanted to spend a brief moment revisiting those dreams as hopefully this time around, they are much clearer, more vibrant, and something you believe by God's grace you can do!

Are you a parent or guardian? There are unique and difficult challenges facing today's youth in addition to the ones they have always faced, especially with regards to their faith. There is no better place to start this process than in your own home and with your own children. What would it look like to be intentional about discipling your kids?

Are you a student or athlete? You likely spend countless hours a year with the same group of people, many of whom you know are struggling in life and faith or who don't know Jesus yet. What would it look like to be intentional about discipling your fellow classmates or teammates?

Are you an employee? Most people spend the majority of their waking time working at their place of employment. In the United States, for example, it is not uncommon for people to spend well over two thousand hours at their job per year. Is there someone at your work you know who is broken, defeated, wandering, or without the Lord? What would it look like to be intentional about discipling your fellow employees?

Are you a small group leader or member? Do you see some of the same people in your church small group each week continually failing to understand their identity in Christ and God-given calling? What would it look like to be intentional about discipling someone in your small group?

Are you a ministry leader or pastor? You are at the tip of the spear for setting the vision and strategy for congregants to be dis-cipled in your church. What would it look like to be intentional about discipling your staff, your lay leadership, or, even better, to help instill a reproducing culture of discipleship that ripples through your church and entire community?

Are you needing to grow as a disciple yourself? Have you been following Jesus but still wrestling with deep questions and doubts? Or struggling to have an impact on those around you or to pray or understand the Scriptures or even just trust God with the little things? What would it look like to be intentional about having a more mature believer disciple you?

Closing Thoughts

Before ending our time together, I wanted to first thank you for taking the time to read and think about this very important subject. I hope it has encouraged and inspired you to take steps in learning to become more like Jesus and help others to do so as well. To wrap up this discussion, I wanted to spend a little time speaking from my heart.

As someone who has engaged in helping to disciple others for almost twenty years, nothing has been more challenging and also more enjoyable and meaningful as this. I have held well-paying desirable jobs and also participated in a variety of church ministries, and nothing even comes close to walking alongside another person and watching God work through you to transform their life! In addition to watching the amazing work of God before my eyes, this process has also resulted in the most significant and meaningful friendships I have ever had. I praise God every day for the privilege to be a part of this Great Commission, and it is my sincerest hope and prayer that you get to experience this as well and that untold numbers of people would be eternally blessed because of it!

I also feel the need to say that, through this experience, my heart has become greatly burdened for the next generation. There exist multitudes of young men and women who are broken, depressed, unnoticed, and wandering without aim or purpose, many within the very walls of our places of worship. Please do not let them persist in this hopeless state. Get over yourself and your seemingly busy schedule and make time to be there for one of these young people. Just imagine what a difference something like that might have made in your life or did make in your life. You can be that for someone else! If you are reading this as one of those young people, know that you don't have to wait, but you can begin this discipleship process with your peers or someone even younger than you, right now! Like the apostle Paul said to Timothy, "Don't let anyone look down on you because you are young, but set an example for the believers in speech, in conduct, in love, in faith and in purity." (1 Timothy 4:12 NIV)

Lastly, on a very practical note, the ideas in this book are not meant to replace the existing ministry activities in your church. Although in some cases, they might influence them. This isn't a new church program or activity for you to sign up for. Hopefully by now, you realize it is an intentional mind-set, an attitude, truly the way all believers are called to live life! So wherever you find yourself, whether it be at work, school, or church, be on the lookout for God-given opportunities. If you are a volunteer in your church's youth program or leading a Bible study, be intentional and invest in the life of someone within that ministry outside of the regularly scheduled events. My hope is that you begin to see traditional church programs as a springboard for some of the most meaningful ministry of your life, **Relational Discipleship**!

As we part ways, I leave you with these words from the apostle Peter and sincerely hope and pray that you, by faith, would lay hold of these great and precious promises given to us by God that we might become like our wonderful master, Jesus!

> His divine power has granted to us all things that pertain to life and godliness, through the knowledge of him who called us to his own glory and excellence, by which he has granted to us his precious and very great promises, so that through them you may become partakers of the divine nature, having escaped from the corruption that is in the world because of sinful desire. (Peter, 2 Peter 1:3–4)

Amen!

Personal Challenge

> ➤ Spend some time reflecting on what part you play in the Body. If you have never done one before, look at taking a spiritual gifts inventory.
> ➤ Prayerfully consider how you can use the time, talent, and treasure that the Lord has blessed you with to encourage others to know and become more like Jesus.
> ➤ Prayerfully make a list of people you want to be intentional about becoming a Paul to and how you are going to approach that.
> ➤ Prayerfully make a list of people you want to be intentional about becoming a Barnabas to and how you are going to approach that.
> ➤ Prayerfully make a list of people you want to be a Paul to you and how you are going to approach that.
> ➤ Reflect on how you are at engaging with different types of relationships. Are you best with momentary relationships, seasonal relationships, or lifetime ones? Come up with a simple plan to be more intentional in engaging people in the way that challenges you the most.

About the Author

Jonathan Engbrecht is a strategic thinker, consultant, mentor, and renaissance man. He has spent nearly twenty years in countless ministry endeavors while simultaneously working as an engineer, mostly in research and development. He holds two degrees in electrical engineering, including a bachelors from the University of Minnesota and a masters from the University of Michigan, Ann Arbor. He is a passionate problem solver, drawing on his broad experience and training in ministry, engineering, and business. Specifically, he has served in megachurch, small congregation, and nonprofit settings in both vocational and volunteer capacities. This includes missions work, youth pastoring, speaking and training, mentoring, facilities management, content development, and worship arts. He has also worked extensively in the tech space, including systems design, software development and architecture, R&D, requirements analysis, and project management.

More recently, he has started consulting with both ministries and tech companies on a variety of subjects. His greatest passion over the years though has been discipling and mentoring the next generation of Christian leaders. He has personally mentored dozens of young men in faith, vocation, and simply life. His other top passion has been using his analytical training as an engineer to help bring creative biblical solutions to address some of the most pressing issues facing the church today. On a personal note, Jonathan also enjoys sports, music, the outdoors, superhero films, and searching for amazing food and beverage experiences!

CPSIA information can be obtained
at www.ICGtesting.com
Printed in the USA
LVHW020840170620
658306LV00003B/751